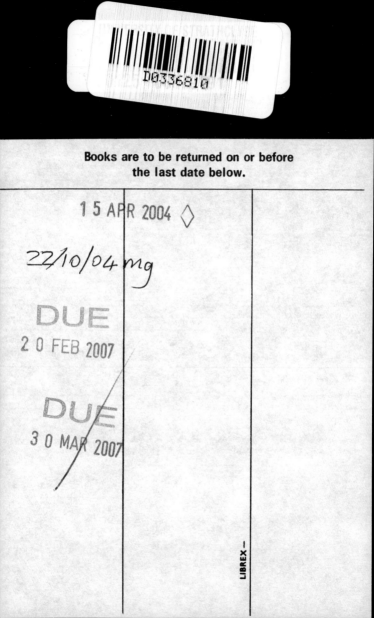

**Books are to be returned on or before
the last date below.**

1 5 APR 2004 ◇

22/10/04 mg

Weightless Wealth

Finding your real value
in a future of intangible assets

Weightless Wealth

Daniel Andriessen

René Tissen

FINANCIAL TIMES

Prentice Hall

An imprint of **Pearson Education**

London / New York / San Francisco / Toronto / Sydney / Tokyo / Singapore
Hong Kong / Cape Town / Madrid / Paris / Milan / Munich / Amsterdam

PEARSON EDUCATION LIMITED

Head Office:
Edinburgh Gate
Harlow CM20 2JE
Tel: +44 (0)1279 623623
Fax: +44 (0)1279 431059

London Office:
128 Long Acre
London WC2E 9AN
Tel: +44 (0)20 7447 2000
Fax: +44 (0)20 7240 5771
Website: www.business-minds.com

First published in Great Britain in 2000

© Daniel Andriessen and René Tissen

ISBN 0 273 64922 1

British Library Cataloguing in Publication Data
A CIP catalogue record for this book can be obtained from the British Library.

10 9 8 7 6 5 4 3 2 1

Typeset by Northern Phototypesetting Co. Ltd, Bolton
Printed and bound in Great Britain by Biddles Ltd, Guildford & King's Lynn

The Publishers' policy is to use paper manufactured from sustainable forests.

About the authors

Daniel Andriessen   As a senior manager of KPMG Knowledge Advisory Services, Daniel Andriessen advises management of international companies in the area of Knowledge Management, Knowledge Organizations, and Knowledge Systems. He has worked as a business consultant for over ten years and is recognized as an expert in the valuation of intangible assets, strategy development, as well as in the implementation of policy simulations and management games.

Daniel Andriessen received his degree in Administrative Science and Social Scientific Research from the Vrije Universiteit (Free University) of Amsterdam and is at the moment finishing his doctoral research on the value of knowledge at Nyenrode University, The Netherlands School of Business.

René Tissen   is managing director of KPMG Knowledge Advisory Services and part-time Professor of Business Management at Nyenrode University. As an international consultant and researcher, he specializes in advising companies on boardroom-level matters of Knowledge Management, Organization, and Human Resources Management. Before joining KPMG, Professor Tissen held a number of executive and senior management positions in both Dutch industry and government as well as abroad.

Acknowledgements

Our special thanks go to Inge van Gisbergen, Prof. dr. Jan Blom, and Martine Frijlink RA, for helping us to create a new way of valuing intangibles. Martine especially has been very instrumental in connecting our general business concepts to current accounting standards and beliefs. Jonathan Ellis, for his ability to grasp the ungraspable and explain the unexplainable and to put our concepts into words. Siemen Jongedijk, for his in-depth research efforts and for finding examples about everything. Our colleagues Steven Olthof, Hennie Both, and Taco van Someren for helping us create a new strategy for Pieces of Fun. The Dutch Ministry of Economic Affairs, especially Arie van der Zwan and Mira Stol-Trip, for providing us with the opportunity to go out-of-the-box. Our clients for allowing us to experiment with new approaches. The board of executives of KPMG The Netherlands, especially Kees van Tilburg for supporting us and giving us the freedom to develop our ideas. And finally at Financial Times Prentice Hall, Angela Lewis, for promoting us and Richard Stagg, for believing in us. Please visit our companion website at www.weightlesswealth.com.

Daniel Andriessen
Dr René Tissen

Contents

Foreword

The authors of *Weightless Wealth* deserve the heartiest congratulations for addressing the long-standing neglect of intangibles in accounting. The difference between the need to act on this problem and what has been done so far has become horrendous. Sound information is essential to effective capital allocation, and effective capital allocation is essential to stable, long-term growth. Without measurements that correspond to value drivers, managers are not going to make decisions that best serve economic growth.

I like to illustrate the problem by citing the ordinary purchase of a cell phone, done every day all over the world. What does the purchaser pay for? Our accounting model tells us the purchaser pays primarily for the physical components and their assembly. But that is hardly the case. A cell phone's physical components are silicon from sand, copper wiring, and petroleum-based plastic. People do not buy cell phones because they want an arrangement of silicon, copper, and plastic. What they are paying for is the knowledge impounded in the cell phone and the knowledge underlying its production. They are paying for the research and development, the design and manufacturing processes, the skills of the workforce, and the software. Investors who want to figure out which of two cell phone makers is going to be most successful are unlikely to focus on their access to silicon, copper, and plastic. They are more likely to focus on the design and features of the companies' products, their rates of improvement, marketing prowess, branding, and research and development programs. These are intangibles, and our accounting model unfortunately is not now well adapted to reflect their values.

The enormous discrepancy between corporate book values and share values in the capital markets cries out for remedy. Managers as much as investors need data that reflects important values. But the problem has not received attention anywhere near commensurate with its dimensions. We can only wonder why.

One possibility is that the focus on international accounting standards has inhibited progress on new approaches to accounting standards. Imaginations have been captured by the idea of uniform accounting by different countries. Impressive institutions, like the World Bank and the IMF, have gotten behind the movement. The need is genuine. In some cases cross-border uniformity under international standards means a great uplift in accounting quality. Nevertheless, the effort may be taking energies that would otherwise go into revising accounting to reflect the newer sources of corporate revenue.

Another possible explanation is that reform finds fewer champions in times of economic plenty than in times of want. People seek solutions when they feel problems, even if the problems are already apparent. Why should investors, for example, demand transformed accounting when they are making money, even if more under the principle that a rising tide lifts all boats than they are willing to acknowledge? The grand ascent of so many stock markets has made many without high-quality information seem well informed enough.

Still another explanation is that the regulators have not shown any interest in reform. That is true in the United States, where the SEC's primary focus has been on tightening the screws on the old accounting model, but I cannot estimate the influence of other regulators around the world.

In the end, of course, the causes of inattention do not matter so much as potential consequences. They argue brutally for giving this subject attention. The greater the discrepancy between share prices and the values foreseeable from relevant, reliable disclosure, the less effective our capital markets. The greater the discrepancy between managers' appreciation of the sources of value and the real sources, the less sure their strategies. If our remarkable period of growth is to continue and be less vulnerable to steep downturns, we need relevant, reliable information about what drives value creation in corporations.

We need practical studies such as this one. Hopefully, it will also stimulate new attitudes. Regulators need to shake their cobwebs; standard setters need to change their priorities; business executives need to reevaluate corporate value drivers; and investors need to see their long-term stake in reformed business reporting and effective corporate management of value drivers.

Robert K. Elliott
Chairman, American Institute of Certified Public Accountants
Partner, Assistant to the Chairman, KPMG LLP
New York, NY, USA

1

When Steven Spielberg, Jeffrey Katzenberg, and David Geffen started DreamWorks SKG, the company had declared assets of $250 million; the market valued the company's shares at $2 billion. After the introduction of Windows 95, Microsoft – an $8 billion company – saw its shares shoot up to $100 billion, making it worth more than either Chrysler or Boeing. Netscape, a $17 million company with just 50 employees, went public and, by the end of the first day, was valued at $3 billion. The average value of all companies traded on the New York Stock Exchange is two and a half times greater than the declared book value. And companies working in information-related fields have a market value on average ten times higher than their book value.

What explanation can be given to this disparity between book value and market value? That is a question which is increasingly concerning managers of companies of all sizes. But an even more important question is how can you, as manager, determine the true value of your company, rather than leaving it to the caprices of the market?

Tom Hoffman has recently been appointed CEO of a well-established company in the toy market called Pieces of Fun. He has taken over from his father-in-law, William Gamble, son of the original founder of the Pieces of Fun, and on the surface it seems a healthy organization. The financial results are good – some would say very good. It has state-of-the-art production machines and factories. And the products are still selling well on the market.

Pieces of Fun originally specialized in jigsaw puzzles. Later it diversified into other areas of what the company called "intelligent entertainment": board games, crossword puzzles, and, most recently, computer games.

On the surface it would seem that Tom has little to worry about. And yet he is ill at ease. He is concerned not so much about the tangible aspects of the business but about the intangible ones.

Three areas give him cause for concern:

■ William Gamble had, during his time with the company, built up a healthy network of contacts in both the publishing and retail branches. Thanks to these contacts, he always managed to get his new products displayed prominently on the shelves of both toyshops and bookshops. Tom is wondering how the organization will manage without this network of contacts.

■ William Gamble was an important father-figure to the staff of his company. He knew what was going on in the business and always had a ready ear for any of his personnel. He knew how to motivate his staff to achieve ever better results. Will the company's culture change with the retirement of William Gamble?

■ The explosive growth of the computer had caused a shift in play. There was a clear move away from the traditional board games towards computer-based games. Will the company have sufficient knowledge and skills to be successful in this new field? And what about finance? It will obviously require deep investments if the company is to become a leader in the field. Is this perhaps a good time to float the company? And if Tom decides to do that, what steps should he take to present the company in the best possible light?

If you look at this fictional example, then you may very well recognize the problems facing Tom. But they are not problems which revolve around tangible matters; rather they deal with the intangibles of a company. Intangibles such as networks, charismatic leadership, culture, skills, competencies, brand, and the like.

> Today, more than at any time in the past, the principal key to any company's success are its intangible assets.

Today, more than at any time in the past, the principal key to any company's success are its intangible assets. But what exactly do we mean by "intangible assets"? The terminology in this field can be very confusing. Some people prefer not to use the word "assets" when talking about intangibles because it reminds them of the meaning accountants place on the word asset: something that is identifiable, is controlled, and clearly distinguishable from an enterprise's goodwill. We will use the term intangibles and intangible assets interchangeably because with "asset" we mean resource or means of production.

⌐ Five types of intangibles

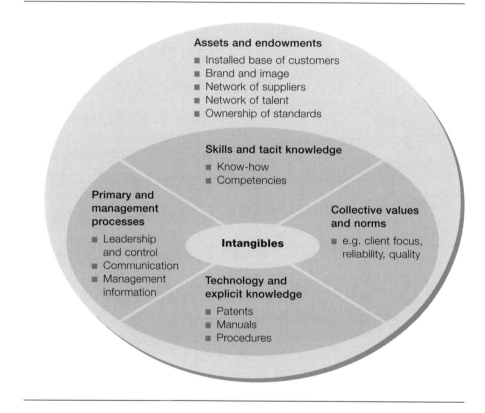

Fig 1.1 ■ Five types of intangibles

Skills and tacit knowledge

The pop singer David Bowie has maintained his career in an industry which is known for "here today and gone tomorrow" for three decades. Much of this, of course, is due to his musical skills. But he also has a tacit knowledge of the mood of the times. The transformations he has undergone from Ziggy Stardust to the White Prince shows an ability to recreate an image in line with the changing tastes of the market. And this proved to be of market value: he became the first person in the entertainment industry to float a personal bond issue. Ownership of the bonds entitles investors to a share in not only the income from royalties on the singer's past material, but also on the receipts of future live concerts. The investors obviously thought it a good deal; the entire issue was sold within one hour for a total cost of over $50 million.[1]

The fact that skills and tacit knowledge are human, rather than company assets, was brought home very clearly to the shareholders of Saatchi & Saatchi, one of the world's leading advertising agencies. In December 1994, institutional investors became annoyed at what they considered the arrogant and reckless behavior of the agency's founder and CEO, Maurice Saatchi. In a protracted battle, the investors forced the board of directors to dismiss him. In protest of this action, several top executives resigned from the company, and this was followed by the defection of several major accounts – first Mars, and then British Airways. The investors considered all this a non-event, for it had little or no impact on the balance sheet. But their action backfired: the stock of the agency, which had been trading on the New York Stock Exchange at 8 fell sharply to 4. The shareholders thought they owned the company; as it turned out, they owned only half of it. The other half of the company was human capital – embodied in Maurice Saatchi.[2]

Collective values and norms

Many companies enjoy success because their employees share collective values and norms. At Microsoft, the culture is so strongly knit, that secretaries who, thanks to their shares in the company, are millionaires, still come into work every morning.

General Motors, in contrast, has never had such an open exchange of information. In fact, until recently, the information culture within the company concentrated mainly on financial information and the personality of the person presenting any new information. A strong product manager was thought able to convince the market of a new model, even if market research had shown otherwise. And many observers believe that this is one of the root causes for General Motors being unable to harness its full potential as a designer and manufacturer of automobiles. The present CEO, Jack Smith, was able to change this culture and now the emphasis lies more firmly on operational and quality information.[3]

Many veteran executives at Nike spend time telling what has become known as "corporate campfire" stories. They believe that the best way for employees to create a prosperous future is to remember a company's past. The stories people tell are not about extraordinary business plans of financial manipulation, but rather about people "getting things done." Stories about getting things done, about keeping promises, about helping athletes achieve their goals. In 1970, Nike began its "Corporate Story Telling Program," which lasted, then, just a single hour; today orientation lasts two days, and begins with the story of Nike's heritage.[4]

Siebel Systems is a company with an intense culture – and this is why it has been able to grow so rapidly. Its present clients include many of Fortune 500 giants such as Ford, Lockhead Martin, Chase Manhattan Bank, and Kellogg. Before Siebel formed his own company he had worked at Oracle – a company which was known for aggressive sales tactics that occasionally rubbed people up the wrong way. Siebel adopted a different strategy: customer relations is so important to the company that 40% of a sales rep's pay is based on customer evaluations rather than on sales commissions. The importance of the customers is further underlined by naming conference rooms for customers. Which explains why Siebel staff members are sometimes heard saying: "Let's meet in Kellogg."[5]

Technology and explicit knowledge

Many companies have their roots in the industrial economy, where considerable emphasis was placed on mechanical technology. As we move into the knowledge economy the focus has shifted towards digital technology and the accumulation of so-called explicit knowledge – the knowledge stored in databases, procedures, and handbooks. More and more companies are trying to manage and exploit this knowledge in a proactive way. The ability to turn such intellectual capital into stand-alone profit-makers has also become a key element to success. This was proved by Dow Chemicals, which was able to create healthy profits with the many patents it has been awarded over the years. Similarly, Montell has also been able to exploit its patents; income from this part of its business is an important source of profit. Royal Philips Electronics is a company with a long history in innovation and research, and has developed more than 60,000 inventions and registered in excess of 10,000 patents. Many of these produce income for the company today.

Primary and management process

Considerable knowledge can be found embedded in primary processes. Enterprise resource planning allows mass use of this intellectual capital, and is increasingly being applied by knowledge-rich companies.

Management processes, too, can be vital in creating cultures which are aware of the importance of knowledge. Ahold, the supermarket giant, has been able to expand world-wide thanks to a culture of trust, open relationships, and decentralized authority. Other multinationals, however, frequently suffer from a bureaucracy which does not help fast and proactive decision-making. At Royal Philips Electronics, the former complex matrix organization – with responsibilities shared by national organizations and product divisions – frequently meant that consensus was hard to achieve and decision-making was a protracted process. At Royal Dutch Shell, the multinational oil company, a recent internal study shows that the Brent Spar affair – which revolved around the disposal of an out-dated oil rig – was largely due to an excess of bureaucracy and centralization within the company.

These findings were additionally emphasized in a recent study which shows that one of the major causes for a company's non-performance can be found in the management style at the corporate headquarters.

It would be wrong, however, to paint too black a picture. Many companies are concentrating on improving the situation. McDonald's, for example, has created a process which allows them to offer the same quality standards throughout the world. And 3M has introduced a new scheme which allows employees to spend some of their time developing new ideas and innovations.

Assets and endowments

This is, perhaps, the most extensive group of intangible assets, covering a whole range of issues such as brand, network of suppliers, talent, and ownership of standards.

Brand and image are two of the most valuable assets a company can own. Many of today's most successful companies enjoy a strong brand reputation – an image achieved thanks to a single-mindedness focus and a long-term strategy of image establishment. Names such as Coca-Cola, Harley-Davidson, McDonald's, Gucci, Nestlé, Unilever, Intel, and Yahoo! are all recognized as market leaders in their own fields. Often the brands have become synonymous with the product itself, such as Coca-Cola. Others have established a reputation as market owner: McDonalds and Yahoo! Some are synonymous with quality, such as Gucci and Unilever, while others are considered at the cutting edge of new technology, such as Intel, which has created its reputation by continually beating the competition to the market with the next generation chips, thus intentionally making their existing generation of processors obsolete. Their competitors have been forced into a position of following the leader and have never been able to achieve the sort of profits or market share which Intel has booked. And people buying a Harley-Davidson do not simply buy a motor bike, they buy into a life-style, which includes clothing, accessories, and after shave. As S. David and Ch. Meyer wrote in *Blur*,[6] "Harley's profit margins are higher than many of its competitors; the premium it earns is for the emotional value it brings to the transaction. And naturally, it's repaid in emotion as well. The degree of loyalty and pride of ownership that Harley riders exhibit is truly phenomenal. How many other products could inspire tough guys to wear conspicuously labelled merchandise?"

A strong brand, however, does not provide total protection in every circumstance. Shell's reputation was considerably damaged during the Brent Spar affair, when Green activists made Shell appear indifferent to environmental issues and finally forced the company into a solution for the disposal of an out-dated oil rig many times more expensive than the initial plan. And today, one of the seemingly invincible brands in the sports wear industry – Nike – is becoming a victim of its own success. How many young people want to wear the same sports shoes as their grandparents? Gucci – now once again a leader fashion label – was faced with a similar problem several years ago, when its image was of a chic but dusty fashion house which had little to do with *haute couture*. Since the arrival of Tom Ford as head designer, however, the company has seen its position reversed, and is now considered by many to be once again on the cutting edge of fashion. The question is how Nike can achieve a similar transformation now that it has established itself so firmly in the market.

One of the problems concerning the CEO of Pieces of Fun in our example at the beginning of this chapter was that with the departure of the former president, the company may lose its network of contacts within its most important market areas. And indeed, as it becomes increasingly difficult – and some would same increasingly undesirable – to do everything "in house," a *network of suppliers* is invaluable.

Sara Lee and Benetton have both built up networks of suppliers which ensure that products are fast to market. And they have both established a fast reporting and logistics system which enables them to adapt their supply to proven market demand. Benneton, in particular, managed, thanks to its network of suppliers and its close contacts with its outlets, to ensure that its shops were stocked with those articles which were selling the best. By using suppliers with a very high level of flexibility, Benetton is able to ship new lines to replace those which were selling less well in a matter of weeks.

A third important asset is an *installed base of customers*. Visa and Mastercard, the major credit card companies, both have a huge installed base of customers. Both are now developing ancillary services which they offer to their existing customers. These include financial services, but also holidays and gifts.

The importance of an installed base of customers is recognized by many companies. Customer loyalty programs are rife and can be seen as a way for companies to lock in their customers to them. Sometimes, this aim can lead to an outright corporate war. Netscape and Microsoft, for example, are currently involved in such a battle, hoping to ensure that customers are "locked in" to their system. The problem here, however, is that the costs of changing from one system to another are so negligible that many people wonder whether a lock-in situation in this market area could ever be achieved.

Scott McNealy of Sun Computers once said that no matter how good your staff are, you have to acknowledge that most of the brightest people don't work for you, won't work for you, and you must organize accordingly. And so a *network of talent* becomes a vitally important asset for any company. Talent which can be involved and used whenever required.

Some regions have become famous for their network of talent. Silicon Valley has the greatest concentration of creative minds in the information technology industry. Every day, ten new millionaires are created there. This enormous depot of talent is not a formal network; rather it is an informal network which creates an environment of creativity which is to the benefit of all the companies working there. A similar situation arose when several dozen bio-tech companies pooled their resources and created the so-called Massachusetts Miracle. The result was not only an environment in which the cross-fertilization of ideas was stimulated, but also one which offered a far better investment climate.

A final asset is the *ownership of standards*. There has been a long history of standard wars, where competing companies – or even countries – have actively lobbied for the acceptance of one standard over the rest. The war between Microsoft and Netscape in the field of web browsers continues unabated. But it is only the latest in a long history of such battles. In the industrial age, there was a battle about the proper railway gauge. There has been a battle – long since ended in stalemate – between the American NTSC television system, the European PAL system, and the French SECAM standard. In mobile digital telephony, there is a growing battle for a world standard, with the principal players being the American CDMA and TDMA systems and the GSM standard, adopted by Europe and the Asian Pacific countries. The battle in video recording – with the Philips-developed V2000 system eventually losing to the Matashusta and JVC VHS system – has resulted in the Japanese industry enjoying on-going profits from world-wide licensing agreements.

Undoubtedly the ownership of standards can form a healthy, if unpredictable, source of on-going income for the company concerned.

⌐ What has brought the change?

Today we are living in the knowledge economy. That economy is no longer of the future, something which is imminent; it is now. The industrial economy, which started at the turn of the 20th century with giants such as Henry Ford and Thomas Edison, laid the emphasis on people as "hands." By the 1980s, however, the first signs of a shift towards a new economy were recognized. The growth in sectors other than those directly involved in manufacture was noticeably greater. There was a clear shift from the industrial economy to the service economy.

Now the economy has shifted again – this time to a knowledge economy. The signs are clear. In the United States, technology-driven companies with a major knowledge component are outgrowing almost every other company: America On-line has grown by 215% in just one year. Mcafee Associates has grown by 110%. While healthcare companies such as Oxford Health Plans and Healthsource have been growing by 130% and 93% respectively. [7] And part of the reason for the success of these companies is that they are all modern start-up companies, that did not have to drag the tradition of industrial operations with them. They were free to act in the knowledge economy in the way best fitted to it.

Many traditionally industrial companies – those designed and built to produce physical products – are being forced to re-think their operations to meet the new challenges of the knowledge economy. Many companies are feeling pressurized, purely for self-preservation, to move into knowledge products and services – without being particularly well-equipped to handle the new demands which are made on them. For example, today's auto industry is almost a part of the electronics industry. The value of the electronic content is higher than that of steel.[8] And not only are more and more functions in the car being controlled and maintained by electronics, the production process is now so highly computerized that it is possible to produce highly customized cars on a single production line. Companies in other fields are also seeing the knowledge content of existing products increasing dramatically. And whether in computers or airlines, again it is electronics which are the enabling factor. For it is the growth of electronics, and the growth of functions which can be handled by electronics, which are changing some products areas beyond recognition.

And then there are companies which are actually moving into producing intangible products. The money industry, for example. And the information industry. In the airline industry today, all the profits are in information. When Galileo, the global airline booking and information system, was floated on the market, it was valued at US$2.45 billion.[9] Reuters, the international news provider, is also growing, thanks to the need in many branches for up-to-date information. It now provides not only news services, but also information aimed specifically at the financial world. It combines data with content and is investing venture capital in start-up companies which are specialized in search engines and data access and manipulation.

> Today, managers who ignore the importance of intangibles for the true value of their companies, are managers who are no longer fit to manage.

So the signs of the knowledge economy are all around us. Seminars and international business meetings are being arranged around the subject of the knowledge economy. It is high on the priority list of every manager. To continue operating today as if you are still in the industrial economy is the recipe for failure.

With the arrival of the knowledge economy, the importance of intangibles has also increased. After all, knowledge, observers maintain, is in the heads of employees, not in the data banks of computers.

Today, managers who ignore the importance of intangibles for the true value of their companies, are managers who are no longer fit to manage.

⌐ The way we value companies is driven by intangible factors

But it is unlikely that any manager could be blind to the effect intangibles have on the way companies are currently valued. There is, as we have already seen, a growing discrepancy between the book value of a company and its market value.

Investment bankers are moving away from valuing a company purely on the published results. In fact, a recent article by Sarah Mavrinac and G. Anthony Siesfeld,[10] showed that when investment bankers were asked which "intangible" aspect of a company they considered most significant in their assessment process, their top five were: execution of corporate strategy; management credibility; quality of corporate strategy; innovativeness; and the ability to attract employees. Mavrinac and Siesfeld further concluded that stock prices are influenced by intangible matters. These include customer satisfaction, TQM (companies showing an "above average implementation" of a Total Quality Management program were rewarded by a share price increase of some 15% in the five years after the start of the program), new product announcements, product quality levels, and employment development programs.

This disparity between a company's book value and its market capitalization has become known as Tobin's Q and has been described by George Gilder in the *Wall Street Journal* as the "index of the entrepreneurial dynamite in a capital stock."[11] When WorldCom tried to acquire MCI, it had about $5 billion in equipment, but a market capitalization of $33 billion (a Q of 6.5).[12] This, however, is no exception which proves the rule; on average the market capitalization of companies quoted on the New York Stock Exchange is two and a half times their book value.

One of the companies which is leading the way in developing ways of placing a value on knowledge is the Swedish-based insurance company, Skandia. In their book *Intellectual Capital*,[13] Leif Edvinsson and Michael S. Malone underline that over the past 20 years, the gap between a company's balance sheet and the value placed on it by investors has been significantly widening. Between 1973 and 1993, the median book-to-market value increased from 0.82 to 1.692. The gap in 1992 indicates that approximately 40% of market value of the average American corporation is missing from the balance sheet. For knowledge-intensive companies, that average is 100%.

Edvinsson and Malone continue: "These distortions are reflected in recent US acquisitions. An examination of the relationship between the price paid for US acquisitions over a thirteen-year period between 1981 and 1993 of some 391 transactions with a median value of $1.9 billion shows that the mean of the price of acquisition-to-book value is 4.4. This indicates that, on average, the real values of the acquired corporations were about four and a half times larger than the values reported in the balance sheets. Acquisition of knowledge-intensive companies had price-to-book values larger than ten."

All this shows how important intangibles are to any company operating today. And you as a manager want – understandably – to be able to put a value on those intangibles. Just as Pieces of Fun would want to present a true picture of their company if they took the step to go public, so you are looking for ways to put a much more realistic figure on the real value of your company. But, Edvinsson and Malone, ask: "Do we have the tools to manage these hidden assets? The simple answer is 'no, we don't.'"

And yet this is becoming increasing necessary. Investors, too, see the importance of an analysis of a company's true worth. In the 1960s and 1970s, about 25% of the differences in stock price changes could be attributed to differences in reported earnings. In the 1980s and 1990s, that figure dropped to less than 10%.[14]

All this underlines that the present means of reporting company value is, for investors, out-dated and insufficient. They are forced to apply other methods of judging a company's value and this leads to volatile markets. For this reason, concludes Baruch Lev "for capital markets to function best, financial statements need to be as informative as possible."[15]

The growth in the value gap has not decreased; if anything, that gap is getting larger all the time. According to David J. Skyrme,[16] the average ratio of market value to book value for companies constituting the Dow Jones Industrial Index was over five. This ratio, however, typically exceeds ten for information or knowledge intensive companies. These include sectors such as software and biotechnology. This difference, explains Skyrme, is "largely made up of intellectual capital: those intangible assets that have real value, but which are not recorded in company accounts. These intangibles include patents, trademarks, know-how, reputation etc."

Margaret Blair, a Brookings Institute economist, also reaches the conclusion that the swing towards greater value being placed today on intangible assets. She calculated the changing relationship between tangible assets (property, plant, and equipment) and total market value for a large number of US manufacturing and mining companies. In 1982, she concluded, tangible assets accounted for 62% of the companies' market value; in 1992, they accounted for just 38%. And these figures, you should remember, are for industrial companies – typically companies which require large investments in tools, equipment, and plants.[17]

Current company measurement systems ignore intangibles

All this means that if you are to be able to put a true value on your company, you need to know more than ever before the value of the intangibles in your company. But the question which arises is how do you calculate that? Today's measurement systems all fall short. When you read your balance sheet, do you really have any idea of the value – the real value – of your company? Does your balance sheet give investors the whole picture? Is your company dramatically undervalued? Can you really trust the market to put a true value to your efforts?

A large part of the problem is that our financial reporting systems are all firmly rooted in the industrial economy, where tangible assets – as Margaret Blair clearly showed – gave a good picture of a company's perfor-mance and expectancies. Even our management terms reflect this industrial mind-set: gearing up for the future, retooling, re-engineering.

But we are no longer in the industrial economy.

Traditional financial reporting concentrates on historical matters. Things which can be measured. Which are static. Which are tangible. They reveal little of the assets which today, in the knowledge economy, play a vital role in the success (and continued success) of the company. Nor do present financial indicators give any true picture of the key factors for success. And a balance sheet says very little about future success.

Yet while financial measurement systems are rooted firmly in the past, investors are concentrating on the future. On growth. On continuity. On the intangible. They arrive at a market valuation by using intuition and assessment processes which are no longer controlled by the company itself. Processes on which you can have little, if any, influence.

It is hardly surprising, therefore, that an increasing number of private and public organizations are calling for a large-scale reform of current financial measurement systems.

Criteria for the treatment of intangibles

Venture capitalist and business writer William Davidow wrote: "There's a need to move to a new level in accounting, one that measures a company's *momentum* in terms of market position, customer loyalty, quality, etc. By not valuing these dynamic perspectives, we are misstating the value of a company as badly as if we were making mistakes in addition."[18]

It is obvious, however, that any new system for calculating a company's current financial situation – which takes into account the intan-gibles we have been discussing – will need to meet a number of criteria. T. H. Donaldson, in his book *The Treatment of Intangibles*,[19] lists four such criteria.

1 Any system should be conservative. It should ascribe a value only to those intangibles which can be justified by sound analysis. If the valuation techniques used can only provide a very rough value – with a large discrepancy between the upper and lower limits – then companies should adopt the lower value for that intangible.

2   Any system should be systematic. It should allow everyone to apply it in the same way. On the other hand, it should give companies sufficient flexibility to make adjustments required by their particular point of view. Nevertheless, the system developed should provide a common starting point.

3   Any system should emphasize value, not costs. This means that the system should allow companies to value the intangible as an asset, whether in terms of cash flow, sales value, or replacement value. The costs for developing or acquiring the intangible asset should be considered an expense, with no necessary connection to its value.

4   Any system should be as accurate as possible within the limitations of any valuation technique. Companies should accept a value at the bottom end of the calculated scale, rather than avoiding making a valuation because there is uncertainty about the precise value. It is better to be approximately right than precisely wrong.

Planning problems

In the knowledge economy, financial systems are notorious for their inability to help provide data for the development of a business plan. Financial data may provide an inexhaustible amount of information about the past, but it doesn't give any indication of the levers you must pull in order to create value for the future. Kutzman supports this view: "Managing by financials won't necessarily get you better financial results, because financials only tell you where you were – they're history. They don't tell you where you're going. And they certainly don't tell you anything about potential."[20]

All this creates an ambiguous situation for you. How do you convince shareholders and investors of the future value-creating potential of your company? If you are unable to place a value on your intangibles, are you then able to give a true picture of your company's future potential? The past is done and gone; the future is where success lies. Yet with today's financial measurement practices, you are being forced to move into the future without so much as a compass, let alone a map. *Trend Monitor International* suggests that measurement systems need to focus on intangibles (not tangibles), the future (not the past), and shift from reductionist/additive measures (as used by accountants) to combinatorial measures.[21]

Today, the need for drastic changes in reporting systems is being fuelled by globalization, new technology, and notions of increased accountability being placed on corporations, professions, and other companies.

What you want is not what you get

A recent survey was held concerning the information needs of 25 of the largest fund managers in the US and Europe; these were then matched against the information provided by 100 of the world's top companies. The results clearly showed that what fund managers want is a lot different from what the companies provide them. One example places the present discrepancy between what is required and what is offered: investors ranked information about intellectual capital very high on their list of requirements, with 68% saying is was extremely important; intellectual capital, however, appeared in only 8% of the annual reports researched.[22]

The need for a radical change in reporting systems is recognized not only by managers but also by accountants. In its study "Towards a market-led reporting model," the *Institute of Chartered Accountants in England and Wales* listed a number of features of the "old" (read current) system and the way they will need to change in a possible "new" system. We will list them in Table 1.1.

The old system	The new system
Shareholder focus	Stakeholder focus
Paper based	Web based
Standardized information	Customized information
Company controlled information on performance and prospects	Information available from a variety of sources
Periodic reporting	Continuous reporting
Distribution of information	Dialog
Financial statements	Broader range of performance measures
Past performance	Greater emphasis on future prospects
Historical cost	Substantial value-based information
Audit of accounts	Assurance of underlying system
Nationally oriented	Globally based
Essentially static system	Continuously changing model
Preparer-led regulations	Satisfying market-place demands

Table 1.1 ■ Difference between old and possible new systems

In the new valuation system discussed in this book, account has been taken of the needs of managers, companies, investors, and accountants. The result is an approach to measuring your company's value drivers which puts you in control and allows you to unlock the value of the intangibles within your company.

So – are you ready to discover the true value of the knowledge in your company? In the following chapter we take a look at some of the existing theories about valuing the intellectual property in your company. We will see how important it is to assess the value of intangibles so that you can get a better insight into how much your company is really worth.

2

At Pieces of Fun, Tom Hoffman, the new CEO, is still working on a new business plan. His formal business training has given him all the necessary disciplines to work creatively with the company's figures. But the information he has to work with only gives him a limited picture of the true potential of the company he has just taken over. Apparently this was enough for his predecessor; Tom, however, wants much more information. After all, he needs information which will help him in the future; the figures at his disposal tell little more than the company's performance in the past.

And the future is what concerns Tom most. The sales figures are good – but will they still be good in six months' time? Large sums of money are being invested in new equipment, computers, and software, but can he really be sure that the investments the company is making are in the right things? He understands the value of personnel, and over the years, the people in the company have been loyal. But will they remain loyal now that he has taken over? Will they accept his new ideas? Or will they look back nostalgically to the times when William Gamble treated them all like one big family? What would happen to the company if a few crucial people decided to look for work elsewhere? What impact would that have on his plans for the future? Would the company be vulnerable? And what about the competition? Have they been able to develop production processes which can threaten the unique cutting technology which put Pieces of Fun ahead of the field? Or have they, perhaps, developed totally new ideas which could make the traditional methods used by Pieces of Fun seem old-fashioned? And what about the customers? Are they still interested in the company's products? Or are they looking for something new? Something which offers entertainment more in line with modern life? And what will they want in three years' time? If Pieces of Fun simply keep giving them more of the same, will they keep coming back? Or will they turn to the competition? Does the name of Pieces of Fun still mean something to present-day customers? Will retailers continue to order their products, simply on their reputation? Or will pressures from their customers – and disappointing sales results – make them look elsewhere?

Tom Hoffman knows that relying on past performance is no guarantee for future success. He needs to think forwards, not backwards. Yet all his training gave him few skills which he could use to assess future performance. Any new direction he may choose to take would obviously require a major capital injection. Would a bank be prepared to offer him capital based on the traditional figures he had on the desk in front of him? Would these financial statements alone be enough to convince a bank to give him a healthy line of credit? Or would they require more information? Information about the company's competitive position. About its customer base. About its potential. And if, as he was considering, he decided to take the company public, would investors see Pieces of Fun as a solid investment? Or would they simply think that going public was a last-ditch attempt to save a company with too many links to the past?

Tom Hoffman is facing the same challenges that you face in your business. He is faced with putting a value on his company which reflects its true potential – not its tangible assets.

From the past to the present, or from the present to the future

Traditional accountancy practices have always worked from the past to the present. The figures you have at your disposal are a history of your past performance. But even today, when there is a growing awareness that the true value of a company extends far beyond the figures on the balance sheet, you are probably still being forced to use this information for your future strategic planning. And all you can do is look at the assets your company has accumulated in the past and hope this gives you information about whether you have been performing well until now.

But such information is of little help when you want to calculate the true value of your company – and today that means the *market* value of your company rather than its *book* value. And as we've already seen, there's a growing disparity between the two.

In *Intellectual Capital*,[1] Stewart is seemingly adamant: a company, he says, is worth exactly what the stock market says it is worth. The market value of a company is the result of a simple sum: price per share × total number of shares outstanding = market value.

"The simplest, and by no means the worst, measure of intellectual capital," Stewart writes, "is the difference between its market value and its book equity ... If Microsoft is worth $85.5 billion and its book value is $6.9 billion, then its intellectual capital is $78.6 billion." But Stewart also has reservations: "If the Federal Reserve Board raises interest rates and Microsoft's stock drops by 5%, does that mean the value of its intellectual capital has dropped, too?"

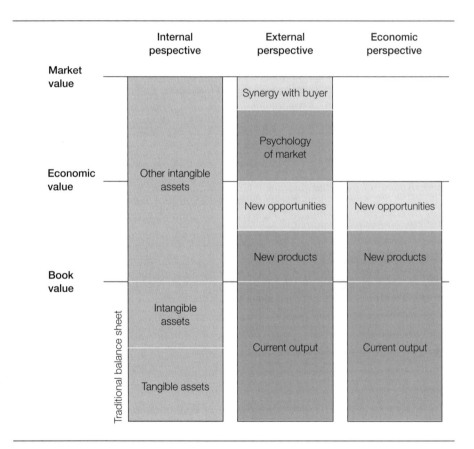

Fig 2.1 ■ Three ways of looking at company value

It is obvious, however, that there is a difference between the way you, as a manager, look at your company and the way the market looks at it. It is all, in fact, a matter of perspective.

For you, as manager, an *internal perspective* of your company is essential. You need to know everything that is going on. You are used to looking at the value of tangible assets from this perspective, and so you would expect the value of the intangible assets – just as the value of the tangible assets – to be independent of future activities. From the internal perspective, the difference between the book value of a company and its market value could be the value of its intangible assets – although Stewart makes a good case for this not being the whole truth. But there are still many managers who believe that the value of a company can be fixed using financial data which is historical by nature.

The opposite view is taken by people outside of the company. For people on the outside, the future prospects are of far greater relevance in their valuation of a company than past performance alone. They are far more interested in deciding whether the company has the potential to continue performing well on a long-term basis. And seen from this *external perspective*, the difference between the book value and the market value of a company revolves around the expected return from present and future products and from perceived opportunities the company may have for entering new market areas.

Today we see that the external perspective is the one used to place a market value on any company. As Stewart writes: "Value is defined by the buyer, not the seller: something is worth what someone is willing to pay for it." If you stare blindly at historical data, you will not be in a position to make any assumptions of what the market may think your company is worth. But then again, you don't want to be taken in by the hypes and fashions of the stock market. You don't want your vision on the true value of your company being blurred by market psychology or by the surplus a potential buyer is willing to pay because of the synergistic effects of a hypothetical merger

> To get a true picture of your company's value, you will need to adopt an *economic* perspective.

To get a true picture of your company's value, you will need to adopt an *economic* perspective, in which the economic value is determined by the future value of your current output, the new products you have in the pipeline and the new opportunities that the future will bring.

And this is what Tom Hoffman is beginning to realize. He is being asked to make decisions about the future based on data from the past. A dilemma being faced daily by every single manager throughout the world.

◻ Creating transparency

The discussion about making the value of intangibles transparent is not, of course, new. The last decades have seen a whole range of attempts to place value on things which, until then, had never been valued separately. In the 1970s, it was people that had to be valued: human resources were recognized as one of a company's major assets, and human resource accounting became increasingly popular. In the 1980s, experiments were made in another area of intangible assets: that of patents and copyrights. The experimental "sale and lease back" formula was developed to help create value from technological knowledge developed by a company and offered to others. In the 1990s, the emphasis shifted to intellectual capital and several companies – notably Skandia, KEMA, and Buckman Laboratories – experimented with ways to make the knowledge in the company transparent.

It is a fact of life that for every action there is a reaction. Progressive thinking – with companies trying to find solutions for the problems of valuing intangibles – was inevitably counterbalanced by conservatives who warned of the dangers of "divulging" information which, to their minds, should remain confidential. The conservatives highlighted the difficulties of substantiating the values attributed to intangibles – could these values actually be proved and was it correct to publish them if they were largely guesswork – while the progressives – determined to make intangibles transparent – developed systems which initially seemed promising (for they allowed the value attributed to the chosen intangibles to be calculated), but which later turned out to offer little extra insight into the true value of the assets under investigation.

◻ Measurement or valuation?

So what about all these methods? Are they really what they claim to be? Do they offer any practical possibilities?

The first thing you notice when reading the many books about valuing intangibles is that they concentrate on the necessity of such a valuation. Even we have fallen into the same trap! But we believe it shows that everybody is agreed on one point: we need a system which allows you to calculate the true value of your own company, rather than allowing external market forces to decide things for you.

It would be wrong, however, to say that there has been no attempt to produce a satisfactory value calculation system. There are, indeed, quite a few practical systems. Yet basically they all fall into two broad categories.

■ *Measurement methods:* these put in indicators which are intended to give managers more insight into the intangibles with their company.

■ *Valuation methods:* these attempt to place a value in monetary terms on the intangibles within a company.

We shall take a look at the most important of these various methods here.

⊔ Measurement methods

Much of the early thinking about measurement methods took place in the late 1980s, so it is hardly surprising that they should rely fairly heavily on techniques which stemmed from the industrial age. Many of the methods use indicators to pinpoint areas of attention. Many of these indicators are similar to those used for measuring production or quality levels. As such, many of the resulting methodologies result in tools for management rather than in information for financial investors; the Skandia Navigator and the Celemi Intangible Assets Monitor come closest to combining these two seemingly diverse aims.

Hubert Saint-Onge model

Hubert Saint-Onge, who was for many years vice-president of learning organization and leadership development at the Canadian Imperial Bank of Commerce, is an important figure in the development of measurement methods for intellectual capital within a company. He believed that a company's intellectual capital was made up of three major elements:

■ *human capital,* which he further described as the ability of people to develop solutions to customer problems;

■ *customer capital,* a total of the penetration of customers within a market, the coverage they had of the specified market, their loyalty to the company concerned, and the profitability which they achieved for the company;

■ *structural capital,* the ability required and the capabilities used to respond efficiently and effectively to market needs.[2]

Much of the ground-breaking work Saint-Onge did was based on his conviction that it is important to understand a company's tacit knowledge, and that by understanding it a manager is better able to achieve a cohesive organization which will lead to performance improvement.

Much of Saint-Onge's work was later used by Leif Edvinsson in the development of the Skandia Navigator.

ICM Model

The ICM Model, developed by Patrick Sullivan, shares many similarities with the Hubert Saint-Onge model: it, too, recognizes the paramount importance of human capital (the company's know-how, including the collective experience, and skills, which is largely not owned by the company) and structural capital (the supporting resources and infrastructure of a company, including all the assets found in the company's financial statement) when investigating the intellectual capital of a company. In addition, Sullivan underlines the importance of intellectual assets (the specific knowledge which a company can own – including its intellectual property, which includes patents, copyrights, trademarks, trade secrets, and semiconductor masks). But the model goes a step further by incorporating what it calls "complementary business assets" – namely, manufacturing, distribution, and sales.

In the model, structural capital is the basis on which all five other "assets" are founded. The three complementary business assets referred to above are all separate from the structural capital base. Human capital, too, is separate, although linked with intellectual assets which penetrate downwards into the structural capital base.

The importance of this model is that it clearly brings to light the relationships within the company and shows the various aspects which together form a company's intellectual capital.[3]

Skandia Navigator

Skandia, the international finance and insurance group, has been investigating the area of Intellectual Capital for many years. In 1991, it appointed Leif Edvinsson as intellectual capital manager, and since then he has done considerable practical work in developing a system to value intellectual capital within an organization, elaborating on the pioneering work of both Hubert Saint-Onge and Patrick Sullivan.

In 1994, Skandia published its first report of intellectual capital as a supplement to its annual report. This was logical, as many investors consider the "footnotes" to a balance sheet to be of far greater importance than the figures themselves. Such footnotes can give indications of matters of importance to the company, rather than just of importance to its financial reporting. This "footnote" information can cover many issues: the acquisition of an important patent; that a key manager has accepted a position elsewhere; or that an operating license has been obtained. As Stewart writes: "In fact, from one perspective, it might be said that the study of intellectual capital is that search for ways to systematically capture, elucidate, and leverage the subjective, half-hidden information about a company now hidden in footnotes to its balance sheet."[4]

Edvinsson states that the capital of a company can be divided into two parts: financial capital and intellectual capital. The financial capital is well reported and documented in the annual report; the intellectual capital, on the other hand, is often the result of "hidden values" and as such is difficult to calculate.

For Skandia, intellectual capital is the sum of human capital (the brains, skills, creativity, persistence, and dedication of the people working in the company) and structural capital (which encompasses everything that remains in the company once the people working there have gone home). This structural capital can be further sub-divided into customer capital (which is not tangible, but nevertheless makes an important contribution to the company) and organizational capital – the structure of the company, the management knowledge, management reporting systems, and so on. This organizational capital can be further divided into innovation capital and process capital.

With this as its background, the Skandia Navigator offers a model in which five areas of *focus* are defined. First there is the *financial focus* – this is the traditional balance sheet and income statement, with its details of the past performance of the company. Then there is the *customer focus*, which addresses all issues concerning a company's customers. Third is *process focus*, which concentrates on the processes which make the company's activities possible and efficient. Fourth is *renewal and development focus*, which involves all those activities such as innovation, R&D, creativity, and ingenuity which are essential in ensuring a sustainable success for a company into the future. It is this future focus which turns Skandia's Navigator from a simple presentation method (which is what most Annual Reports are) into a method which navigates the future.

The fifth, and most important, area of focus is *human focus*. And it is not without reason that this is seen as the very heart of all activities embraced under the term "intellectual capital." For the human factor is vital within any company. People have ideas; they carry them around with them and take them with them when they go home or if they leave to accept a job elsewhere. Thus human focus is the link between the other four areas; it forms the heart of all discussions within Skandia about intellectual capital.

The Skandia Navigator, developed by Edvinsson, looks at the intellectual capital within a company from a "value creation" view. As we said in our previous book,[5] companies today must realize that they are not in the business of creating knowledge; they are in the business of creating value. For this reason – and because, as it is stated, the Skandia Navigator is *not* designed to determine market value, but rather to give managers a broader perspective for making decisions – it should be seen as an important management tool, rather than as a tool to determine the value of intangibles within a company. The Skandia Navigator brings to the surface information on "hidden values" which may otherwise remain buried, without attributing a value to these intangibles; rather it provides information which exists as a supplement to financial statements rather than produce figures which can be integrated into traditional financing methods. It provides managers with a better understanding of the true nature and value of the company without reaching an accountable value at the end. And for this reason, its aims are different to those of the method developed by us and explained in the later part of this book.

IC Index™

The IC Index™ was originally developed by the London-based Intellectual Capital Services. It suggests that companies define a series of indicators for key operations within their companies, so that changes can be monitored and strategic decisions can be taken based on the different figures given to each index.

Johan Roos and Göran Roos have developed this idea further, into what they call "the second generation" of IC practices,[6] which consolidates the various indicators into one single IC Index™.

Johan Roos believes that any measurement of IC should be clearly linked to company operations and provide managers with indicators for strategic planning.

"The most critical question most managers wish to have answered is what knowledge has an impact on earning capacity. Market value is a function of estimated cash-flow; profit is a matter of opinion, cash is a matter of fact. And where does it come from? Basically two sources: the cash flow generated today, and the opportunities. And where do these opportunities come from? Initially from the human imagination. Intellectual Capital is the manifestation of the opportunities stemming from human imagination. And ultimately the differences in market value will be determined by Intellectual Capital."[7]

For this reason, Roos believes that it is of utmost importance that any indicator of intellectual capital should show flow. Until now, he maintains, the methods developed for placing a value on the intellectual capital in a company are static, offering just a snapshot of a moment of time. "Flow indicators," he writes, "convey much more information than stocks can alone."[8]

In order to consolidate all the various indicators which a company may have developed into a single figure, it is first necessary to review all the indicators a company has in place and decide what information the indicator is supposed to show, what it actually measures, and how understanding the change in the figures produced by this indicator will be useful for strategic planning purposes. For each area of intellectual capital – and Roos believes there are a number of strategically important areas which he calls relationships, human capital, infrastructure, and innovation – a number of indicators should be put in place, each of them "weighted" according to three factors: the strategy, the characteristics of the company, and the characteristics of the industry in which the company operates.[9]

Roos gives an example of a series of indicators for each of the four areas which were put in place by a bank which looks like this:

Relationship capital index

- Growth in number of relationships
- Growth in trust
- Customer retention
- Distribution channel productivity and quality

Human capital index

- Fulfillment of key success factors
- Value creation per employee
- Training efficiency and effectiveness

Infrastructure capital index

- Efficiency
- Effectiveness
- Key success factor utilization
- Distribution efficiency

Innovation capital index

- Ability to generate new business
- Ability to generate good products
- Growth
- Ability to productify.

By using each of the indicators per area, an index can be produced for that area, and by consolidating the four together, an IC Index can be reached for the total operations. In this way, deviations in each of the areas can be plotted separately, while at the same time allowing a helicopter view of the total operations. This is important for strategic purposes, for the figures provide valuable information to managers when they are faced with a choice between various options: by projecting results based on the indicators into the future, managers can see what effect their decisions will have on the overall IC Index of the company. This approach also allows incidental actions to be placed in a proper perspective. As Roos says: "Not all changes in the knowledge base will impact your earnings capacity. Simply hiring Einstein will not make your company richer!"[10]

The IC Index™ is a valuable strategic tool, allowing managers better insight into the consequences of their decisions. To quote Roos: "The main benefit of an IC-Index is making uncertain and subjective feelings about what is happening in the company more visible, thus forcing management to discuss the issues and come up with a solution."[11]

Balanced scorecard

One of the managerial stumbling-blocks referred to by Roos – the proliferation of performances indicators and measurements – had already been highlighted in 1992 by Robert S. Kaplan and David P. Norton in their discussion of their balanced scorecard approach.[12] In fact they quote one manager as saying that the on-going introduction of new measurements in his company was referred to as the "kill another tree program."[13]

The aim of the balanced scorecard is to allow managers to look at their business from four important perspectives:

- *Customer perspective:* how do customers see us?
- *Internal perspective:* what must we excel at?
- *Innovation and learning perspective:* can we continue to improve and create value?
- *Financial perspective:* how do we look to our shareholders?

Managers are able to list for each of these areas their specific goals and to decide which measurements are required to show how these aims are being met. By asking managers to concentrate on major strategic issues, the balanced scorecard has a positive effect on reducing the number of performance indicators required within a company.

27

The advantage of this approach is that it can be fully geared to the company's needs. If, for example, a company decides that customer satisfaction depends on prompt delivery, then an indicator to show how delivery times are met and improved can be incorporated. This indicator can then be coupled with a process indicator, which measures the internal perspective of a company's delivery program, a training indicator, showing what measures have been taken to improve delivery logistics, and finally to an indicator which shows how this affects the financial perspective.

> This ability to see the whole picture, rather than concentrating purely on improvements in one area, is at the heart of the balanced scorecard approach.

This ability to see the whole picture, rather than concentrating purely on improvements in one area, is at the heart of the balanced scorecard approach. And since it is aimed primarily at providing management with a tool by which it can plan strategy and judge the results it achieves, it is more a signalling device than a valuation tool. For this reason, it breaks with the notion that performance indicators are purely intended for control of processes. As Kaplan and Norton write: "The scorecard puts strategy and vision, not control, at the center. It establishes goals but assumes that people will adopt whatever behaviors and take whatever actions are necessary to arrive at these goals."[14]

Intangible assets monitor

The intangible assets monitor, developed by the Swede Dr Karl-Erik Sveiby in the mid-1980s, shows many similarities with the later balanced scorecard. It defines three areas of importance when determining the intangible assets of a company: external structure, internal structure, and people's competencies, which are very similar to the customer perspective, the internal business process perspective, and the learning and growth perspective of the balanced scorecard. Yet there are several fundamental differences between the two independently developed methods.

The fundamental difference is that Sveiby is convinced that people are an organization's only profit generators. The profits resulting from the actions of those people – whether products, services, patents, copyrights, and the like – are indications of the success of a company; but it is people who make this happen, and must therefore be considered the generator of all profits within a company. According to Sveiby[15] "human actions are converted into both tangible and intangible knowledge 'structures,' which are directed outwards (external structures) or inwards (internal structures)." And he further concludes: "These structures are *assets* because they affect the revenue streams." This is an assumption which is not included in the thinking of the balanced scorecard approach. In fact, the balanced scorecard, which has its roots in traditional industrial thinking, actually regards people as costs, rather than revenue creators and ignores Sveiby's conviction that people are the only generators of revenue which a company possesses.

Nor does the balanced scorecard pay any attention to the question: What constitutes the company? Rather, Kaplan and Norton take this as a given, and see their tool as a way of providing management with a method which complements the financial measurements of past performance with measures which indicate the drivers of future performance. Sveiby clearly approaches the whole matter from a knowledge perspective; Kaplan and Norton approach it from a management vision perspective.

Unlike the balanced scorecard, Sveiby's intangible assets monitor does not include a financial measurement. And this is a result of his underlying conviction that "human knowledge has very little to do with money, and very few people handle money. If the notion of people as revenue creators is reasonably correct, we therefore have to come closer to the 'source' of their knowledge if we wish to measure it more accurately."[16]

The similarities between the balanced scorecard and the intangible assets monitor has resulted in a degree of confusion among analysts of knowledge measurement systems. Some see the Skandia Navigator as a direct result of Sveiby's research; others see the Navigator as an approach which combines the two systems into one. Whichever is true, it is indisputable that both the balanced scorecard and the intangible assets monitor have had enormous influence on encouraging managers to look further than the hard figures of their financial statements when assessing the value of their company.

Celemi Intangible Assets Monitor

Celemi, with headquarters in Sweden and operations throughout the United States and Europe, is an international knowledge company which creates learning processes. Using the results of research work done by Karl-Erik Sveiby, it has produced a business simulation model for knowledge companies called Tango™. Using this model, it has undertaken two intangible assets audits of its own operations, the results of which were published with the financial statements.

The Celemi Intangible Assets Monitor defines three areas of intangible assets: *our customers* – which refers to the external structures of relationships with customers and suppliers, brand names, trademarks, contracts and reputation or image; *our organization* – which refers to the internal corporate structure consisting of patents, concepts, vendor contracts, models and computer and administrative systems; and *our people* – which refers to the combined competence of Celemi's employees, such as their ability to act in a wide variety of situations.[17]

Within each of the three areas, Celemi has defined a number of important matters which, it is convinced, play a vital role in adding to the "intangible balance sheet." For customers, for example, Celemi looks further than simply the revenue which is earned from them. Three categories of customers are defined, one for each of the structures – external, internal, and competencies – which are at the core of Celemi's thinking. The number of customers falling into each group gives an indication of the "intangible value" of the customers within the portfolio. These three categories are:

- *Image-enhancing customers* – customers who are well-regarded in the industry and who perhaps can provide testimonials are important in attracting other such customers. Such customers improve Celemi's external structure.

- *Organization-enhancing customers* – customers who demand solutions which are new to Celemi, and thus require the company to adopt new and improved working methods. This customer group improves Celemi's internal structure.

- *Competence-enhancing customers* – customers who require Celemi employees to develop new skills in order to provide the services or products required. These customers help build the employees' competencies.

Several additional indicators have been put in place which help to gain a good impression of, say, the stability of the customer base. Repeat orders, for example, show not only continued customer satisfaction, but also the level of loyalty. Customers who have been with a company for a longer period of time are valuable assets, since acquisition costs for such clients are low. Stimulating growth with existing customers is one of the most cost-effective ways of achieving revenue improvement.

Indicators put in place for the internal organization include figures on seniority and a so-called "rookie rating" – the number of employees with the company for less than a year. A high rookie rating means that there is a higher degree of instability within the company, and it is accompanied by high recruitment costs. Ideally, the rookie rating should be low. In 1996, Celemi had a rookie rating of 68% – a very high figure indeed. But the reason for this was that the company was in the process of transforming itself from a small firm to a multinational company and was being given large projects by its customers. These two factors resulted in the need to recruit large numbers of new employees. It was seen by Celemi as a passing phase, and so the rookie rating was placed in a wider perspective. This highlights an important issue when developing a system for indicating intangibles: management should be provided with valuable information which helps them better understand the way the business is developing, rather than give a static idea of what the business has achieved in the past.

The Celemi Intangible Assets Monitor is issued as an appendix to the financial statement. It lists the findings and – more importantly – includes explanatory footnotes which allow the management to give their interpretation of the figures. These footnotes are an important part of the total monitor, which is intended to give stakeholders in the company a clearer picture of its true value.

Valuation methods

Does a company possess – own – knowledge? Or is it in the heads of the people it employs? Certainly there is some knowledge which a company can claim to own – patents, copyrights, licenses, trademarks, and so on – and such knowledge is called intellectual property. This is, however, knowledge which can be transferred between companies. One company can "sell" the knowledge to another for a fee. This is the case, for example, with patents: the patent-owner can allow another party to make use of the intellectual knowledge contained in that patent for a fee. Such intellectual property can prove a healthy source of income for many companies – consider the licensing fees earned by General Electric or JVC, or the fees shared by Sony and Philips for their patents on CD technology – and for this reason, the tax authorities are particularly interested in earnings which arise from such agreements. The Internal Revenue Service of the US Treasury has approved three methods of valuing such intellectual property.[18]

- The replacement value, when it concerns knowledge which is conventional and routine.

- Payments made for the use of intellectual property in similar situations. This method is applied when the replacement value cannot be accurately calculated.

- Income from licensing, which is calculated against income from similar activities. This method is also applied when the replacement value cannot be calculated.

Such methods are perfectly satisfactory when a tangible product or marketable technology is involved. But knowledge, as such, need not necessarily be tangible – and we have seen that intangible assets are those which most urgently require a satisfactory and reliable valuation system.

It is obvious that much of the knowledge that a company has resides in the heads of its employees. Tapping this knowledge is a major challenge facing every organization. As Frank Carrubba, at the time Senior Vice-President of Royal Philips Electronics, once said: "The trouble with Philips is that Philips doesn't know what Philips knows." And what he meant was that there was a wealth of knowledge in people's minds which was never exploited. Yet it is ultimately the knowledge of the employees – your employees – which adds value to your company. As Jan Timmer, ex-President of Philips, once said: "Philips makes products, but people make Philips." And for "Philips" you can fill in the name of any company you like. Even your own!

Human resource accounting

Following this train of thought it is understandable that valuing knowledge in a company goes hand in hand with valuing the people in a company. And for this reason, there was, for several years, a noticeable trend towards developing methods for "human resource accounting" (HRA).

At the moment, such HRA methods approach the subject from two seemingly contradictory viewpoints: the first from the costs involved in employing people – wage costs, training costs, office or factory space, and so on; the second from the return which the employees generate.

J. Bulte analyzed many of the current HRA methods[19] and came to the conclusion that the greatest difficulty with all the current approaches is deciding exactly what the costs are or returns are. "It is almost impossible," writes Bulte, "to calculate the economic value of labor in isolation. Many aspects of the production process are so inter-linked, that it is almost impossible to attribute the costs or returns to any single entity."[20]

A second problem which he sees is that frequently such HRA methods link profitability with labor. "Many models assume that what is good for an employee – or at least, what the employees consider good for themselves – is automatically good for the company's profitability. Some say: employees want to participate; make such participation possible and the company results will improve."

Another suggested method for calculating the value to the human factor is to attribute any surplus profit to labor. This surplus profit is the difference between the profit made by the specific company compared to that made on average by other companies in the same sector. Let us say that the average profit for a particular sector is 8% on invested capital. This would imply that every company would "earn" $8,000 on every $100,000 it has in invested capital. If a company has an actual profit of $15,000, then its surplus capital is $7,000. The value of labor can now be calculated as follows: $7,000 × 100/8 = $87,500. Although such a calculation may seem elegant, it chooses to ignore any other factors which could be responsible for surplus profit, and therefore should, according to Bulte, be rejected.

Human asset accounting

Similar objections can be made against another method, which uses the goodwill in a company as an indicator of the value of labor. This method, which was proposed by the Institute of Personnel Management and the Institute of Cost and Management Accountants in a publication entitled *Human Asset Accounting*, stipulates that the "goodwill value" is the difference between the potential value of a company (that is, the present value of future profits) and its intrinsic value. The goodwill is then allocated to the various production assets according to the investments made in them. This goodwill is, according to the two institutes, the maximum value which can be attributed to the value of labor; the actual value is calculated by deducting certain other factors – such as returns on patents and long-term contracts, customer loyalty, and so on – and the resulting amount is divided by the total wage costs paid to employees. The figure resulting from this division is called a "gross multiplier," which can be used as an indicator of the profitability of investments. When an investment is made in employees, then the value of labor will increase by an amount equal to the investment multiplied by the gross multiplier. A gross multiplier can also be calculated for smaller groups of personnel. Unfortunately, the whole process is relatively subjective, and seems to be an attempt to create a method in which you design what you want to know at a later date.

The KEMA method

Obviously many of the methods described earlier in this chapter – in particular the Skandia Navigator – owe much to HRA ideas. Some companies, however, have taken the step of including the "value" of employees in the Annual Report. One of the first of these was KEMA, the Dutch Institute for Quality Standards. In its 1994 Annual Report it included a "Knowledge Balance Sheet" with which it tried to show the value of the people and their knowledge within the company. This balance sheet – which was included as a separate table – uses a calculation method based on the replacement value of intangible assets. The figures are calculated using the costs involved in acquiring knowledge and skills – training, education, experience acquired both within the organization and outside it – and the value of the knowledge in the company, including that catalogued in reports and such. The method applied by KEMA places a historical value on assets, but also considers knowledge an asset which decreases in value by 20% per year. The calculations in 1994 resulted in a figure for the value of the company knowledge of Dfl.700 million; the book value of the company's assets in that year was just Dfl.180 million.

The figures just quoted may seem good – after all, the total profits of KEMA in 1994 were Dfl.19.8 million which, based on the declared assets of Dfl.78 million, is relatively good. However, a survey was carried out in the United States which compared the results of KEMA to those of similar knowledge intensive companies operating there. The results showed that the average market value of such companies was, on average, one half of the companies' declared turnovers. In 1994, KEMA had a turnover of Dfl.276 million, which means that the market value – if we apply the figures for American companies – was around Dfl.140 million. If the value of the knowledge within the company was Dfl.700 million, then this implies a return of just 20% on the knowledge. And this can be considered very low. There are two explanations for this: first, that much of the accumulated knowledge within KEMA is not used within the present market; and second, that the knowledge which is used is not used very efficiently.

Knowledge earnings

A final valuation method we should like to mention here is that developed by Baruch Lev. In the article *New Math for a New Economy*,[21] Lev describes his method as follows: "I've developed a way to measure knowledge assets, intellectual earnings, and knowledge earnings. It's a computation that starts with what I call 'normalized earnings' – a measure that's based on past and future earnings … My method looks at the past. But I also look at the consensus forecasts of analysts. Based on those forecasts, I create an average, and I call that normalized earnings. From these normalized earnings, I then subtract an average return on physical and financial assets, based on the theory that these are substitutable assets … and I define what remains as the knowledge earnings."

Lev has applied his method to several companies. Microsoft, according to Lev's calculations, has knowledge assets worth $211 billion. Intel has knowledge assets worth $170 billion, and Merck & Co has knowledge assets worth $110 billion.

A new economy demands new methods

If we look at the various methods discussed here, then we can see that the majority fall short in a number of areas. And perhaps this is because many of them are still rooted in thinking which may have been applicable in the industrial economy, but which have little relevance in today's knowledge economy.

For this reason, we are prepared to stick our necks out and list the disadvantages which we believe adhere to many measurement and valuation methods, while at the same time acknowledging the importance of the various methods in developing our own method called the Value Explorer®.

With this in mind, let us list what we consider to be the disadvantages of the various measurement methods:

- There is little or no connection between the various indicators.
- Most look at each intangible in isolation, where in truth the strength of intangibles is cumulative.
- They fail to show the importance of the various intangibles for the present and future success of a company.

Valuation methods, in our view, also show several disadvantages:

- They generally concentrate on one single intangible and, once again, ignore the interaction between the various intangibles which, for most companies, result in something which is more than simply a sum of the parts.
- They are based on historical data, costs, and past activities, and thus give little indication of the future economic potential within a company.

In other words, applying any of the present methods could provide you with interesting information – but we doubt whether it would be particularly useful to you in your daily business activities. You already know the past; the future is where your true opportunities lie.

Survey the future rather than plot the past

When we were developing the Value Explorer, we realized that there was little need for yet another method of helping you learn what you already know. And this is why we drew up a list of requirements for our new method. We offer them here without further comment.

- Any valuation method should be based on future earnings. This is the life-blood of a company; it is what you are concerned with.

- The method should not restrict itself to quantitative benchmarking or indexes, but should result in a valuation – it should put a number on it.

- Valuation should not be affected in any way by temporary external market influences. It should disregard matters such as day-to-day market psychology, rumors, stock market dynamics, and other matters over which you, as a manager, have little or no control. You can't control the world; you have your hands full controlling your company.

- It would be wrong to look at each intangible in isolation. We have to recognize that the true value of a company lies in the synergy created by all the various intangibles and tangibles. Any valuation should take this combined synergy into account.

- We must realize that knowledge, as such, has no value at all. Today, too many companies are frantically gathering knowledge in the hope that the more knowledge they have, the more successful they will be. But knowledge only becomes a powerful weapon for your company when you learn to use it to add value to your customers. For this reason, knowledge can never exist in a vacuum; it needs other intangibles (and indeed tangibles) such as management processes, collective values and norms, image, branding – all the things we discussed in the opening chapter.

- Every company is – and should be – unique. As a manager you're not anxious to become yet another carbon-copy of your most successful competitor; you want your company to be the best there is. We had no intention of designing a system which would assume that every company is the same – simply because they are not. On the other hand, it is important that any valuation system should allow comparison between companies. So our aim was to design a system which could be tailor-made to specific circumstances – *your* circumstances – while at the same time providing you with a result which would allow you to benchmark your performance with that of your competitors.

■ And most importantly – we wanted our method to give you the help and information you need to be able to leverage the potential of your intangible resources.

Have we been successful? Decide for yourself in the next chapters.

3

Examine your core

At Pieces of Fun, the new CEO, Tom Hoffman, has reached a simple conclusion: his company is unique. History has shown that there is a profitable market for his company's products. But Tom knows that under his management he will be expected to maintain the company's position and even increase it.

As he sat at his desk, he realized that simply saying his company was "unique" was not enough. His customers wouldn't buy more products because he shouted "We are unique." He knew they would reply "The proof of the puzzle is in the playing" – or words to that effect!

Yet Tom knew that being unique – and retaining that unique position in the over-full shelves of toyshops throughout the world – was essential in today's high competitive games market. But he also realized that it wasn't something that just happened. It had to be worked on. And to be able to work on it efficiently, he needed to discover exactly what it was that made Pieces of Fun so unique. He needed to penetrate to the very core of his company. He needed to uncover that core – the soul of the company, he thought, with a smile on his lips – and then design a strategy which would exploit the core of the company and guarantee a continued uniqueness.

Mission statement

As he began his deliberations, he reached for the Mission Statement of Pieces of Fun which he had drawn up with the rest of his key employees. He read it for what must have been the thousandth time – even though by now he knew it from memory.

Our Mission

We will provide intellectual entertainment throughout the world with a competitive product.

We will be creators.

We will design and will offer high craftsmanship using traditional and multi-media carriers.

We are unique and provide added educational value.

We care for people and seek positive challenges.

⌐ The importance of a mission statement

Mission statements have become common in today's business world. Initially many of them were drafted to help motivate employees. It gave them an insight into the direction their company was taking and the contribution they could make to the success of their company. Today, almost every self-respecting company has drafted its own mission statement.

Unfortunately, few of these mission statements actually play a role in strategic thinking. And this is a pity. Certainly a mission statement can help focus thought and attention towards new opportunities. Let us look at an example.

Two successful door manufacturers both decided to draw up their mission statement. It had to be motivating and challenging, while at the same time directing attention at the core business. The first company created a mission statement which said: "We aim to provide our clients with the best doors available in the industry today, manufactured to the highest quality standards, using the best materials and technologies, and meeting the specifications of our customers." The company all agreed with this statement and geared their strategy to achieve their aims. They are still a highly successful door company.

The second door manufacturer, however, went further: it analyzed the market, researched customer requirements, and designed its mission statement to lay the foundation for its future business. It read: "We aim to provide our customers with the best entrance technology available in the industry today, manufactured to the highest quality standards, using the best materials and technologies, and meeting the specifications of our customers."

By replacing the word "doors" by the words "entrance technology," the company widened its vision and its field of operations. Not only did it provide doors, it also diversified into areas such as personal recognition, key cards, security, and electronic surveillance. It is now the world leader in the field, with a turnover many times greater than its former competitor, who is still a manufacturer of doors. And nothing more.

Mission statements are important for business

Arie de Geus, former strategic planner at Royal Dutch Shell, wrote in his book *The Living Company*[1]. "Missions statements are often justifiably criticized because they don't seem to say anything once all the abstractions are in place. But the phenomenon of this abstraction is worth nothing; it is so consistent, from company to company, that it must exist for a reason." This reason, he believes, is that everybody in business knows in his or her heart that too narrow or specific a definition can be literally life threatening. "For long-term survival," he concludes, "a company cannot be defined in terms of the business which it happens to be doing at this very moment."

Amazon.com is a very good example of a company whose mission statement looks further than its present business. Although Amazon.com has become synonymous with books, its mission statement avoids that word altogether. The mission statement reads: "To be the customer's first choice in finding and discovering anything they want to buy online." It does not limit the company to a product or service – except that it is clearly linked to online services. A recent press release from Amazon.com shows how well this strategy is working. We quote: "I'm excited to tell you that we've opened Amazon.com Auctions. Auctions is something completely different for Amazon.com. In the past, when you bought something at our store, you were always buying directly from us. Now, with Auctions, our community of almost 8 million customers can sell anything they want to on the Amazon.com Web site. Letting millions of sellers participate at Amazon.com is another way for us to give you the broadest selection. You'll find rare books and signed first editions, rare music, vintage toys, antiques, sports memorabilia, collectibles of all kinds, etc. etc." Would they have introduced Auctions if they simply aspired to being the best on-line bookstore? We doubt it.

One area which is undergoing constant change is that of communications. Traditionally companies thought people would require two communication networks: a telephone network, which offers high quality voice communications, and a data network, such as internet. Cisco is a company which is breaking away from this duality. Its mission: Powering the Internet, Empowering Humanity. Their goal is to build an infrastructure that combines the precision of telephone networks with the adaptability of data networks.

> For some companies the mission statement encapsulates their strategy; for others it is simply a piece of paper, drafted in a moment of passion, then forgotten.

Perhaps the most remarkable transformation of a company has taken place in Finland. There a company dating from 1865, when it operated a wood-pulp mill and was involved in paper manufacture, has moved into telephony and is now the undisputed leader in mobile telephony: Nokia. Its mission statement is simply its business slogan: Connecting People. This it did initially with wireless and wireline telecommunications and is now integrating a whole range of services into a single product. Recently it unveiled a device which lets you watch TV, surf the Net, send email – and telephone throughout the world.

What is obvious from these examples is that for some companies the mission statement encapsulates the strategy of the company and is constantly in the mind when thinking about alternative directions, while for others it is simply a piece of paper which is drafted in a moment of passion – and then forgotten.

Perhaps it is worth you looking out your mission statement and use it to analyze your company – just as Tom Hoffman did.

⊡ From mission statement to key qualities

In his office at Pieces of Fun, Tom Hoffman is re-reading his company's mission statement. His eye kept returning to a word at the end: unique. We say Pieces of Fun are unique, Hoffman thought, but we don't say what *makes* us unique.

Pulling a piece of paper towards him, he started jotting down aspects of his company which, in his mind, made it unique.

The first thing which came to his mind was their technological competence in the field of printing and die-cutting puzzles. He knew that Pieces of Fun were unequalled in the market in this area. It had always been a source of pride for the company – and he knew it could very well be put to great use in the future.

The second thing which came to mind was the content of the games themselves. Pieces of Fun had always produced games which were challenging and had the unique quality of getting people to become fascinated in them. People wanted to be challenged, he knew, and his company's games not only challenged them, but taught them things as well. It was this, he knew, which contributed to the reputation Pieces of Fun enjoyed as being "unique."

As he thought further, Hoffman realized that this reputation was a third strong point: Pieces of Fun were seen by the market as the company which provided intellectual and challenging entertainment. This was something he had frequently heard from his clients.

As he swivelled his chair round to look out of the window of his office, he realized there was a fourth strength – and that was in the company's structure. It was a family company. Everybody knew everybody else which made communication easy and direct. There was little talk of a hierarchy – everybody felt they were part of the company and were appreciated for their contribution to its success. This, Hoffman knew, was largely due to the way his father-in-law had run the business for so many years. He had encouraged the family feeling which, Hoffman recognized, was part and parcel of the company's uniqueness.

Focus on intangibles

What Tom Hoffman had done was to focus on intangibles. These, as we have just seen, are what make a company unique.

Of course, there are, as we have seen in our first chapter, a large number of intangibles. And while many of these may exist in a company (in fact, the majority will exist in a company, whether you realize it or not), not all of them are equally important. What we need to do is track down those intangibles which add value to the company.

> In the first step towards establishing the economic potential of a company, we have to decide which intangibles are the most relevant to us.

In the first step towards establishing the economic potential of a company, we have to decide which intangibles are the most relevant to us. Not only to find out the economic value of a company – although this is obviously important within the context of the present book – but because those intangibles which add value to your company are the ones which are of strategic importance to your future success.

Such intangibles, however, should never be viewed in isolation. It is only when they combine that the economic synergy is created.

All this brings us to the critical question: how do you decide which of the many intangibles within your company are of strategic importance? And the answer is to define core competencies of your company.

What is a core competence?

It would be easy for most managers to produce a whole list of capabilities which they believe are vital to the success of their company. You could do it without too much effort. Yet such a list will be of only passing interest; it will do little to help you focus on what is of vital importance to the competitive success of your company. It may very well contain valuable information about general capabilities, but it is little more than an initial list which features capabilities, and both core and non-core competencies.

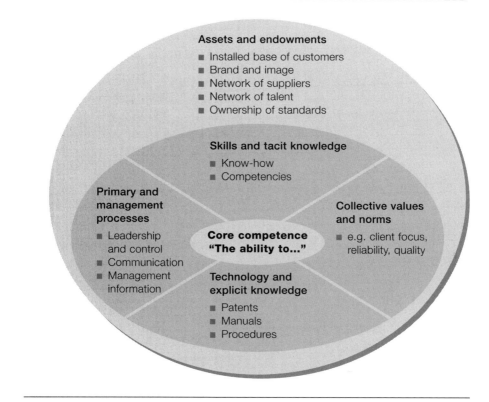

Fig 3.1 ■ Break down of a core competence into its contributing intangibles

So how do you decide your company's true core competencies?

Gary Hamel, in his major work on this subject,[2] first defines what a core competence is *not*. It is not, according to Hamel, an integration of skills – although undoubtedly skills can be a contributing factor to the core competence – nor is it an asset in the accounting definition of the word. It is, he believes, a skill cluster which lies at the center of competitive success and which contributes to the long-term corporate prosperity.

To be considered a core competence, Hamel maintains that any "skill cluster" must meet three tests:

- It must make a disproportionate contribution to customer-perceived value. A core competence must place a company in a unique position to offer a customer benefit. This can range from user-friendliness (something which Apple has promoted very strongly), reliability, range, and so on. McDonald's, for example, produces fast-food quickly and to a constant standard. Honda produces cars with exceptionally fine engines. It is therefore important to ask yourself what your customer really wants. Thus a core competence will almost certainly reflect a core customer benefit.

- A core competence must place the company in a position to be unique. It must offer competitive distinction. For many years, Volvo positioned their cars as "safe." Today, however, the vast majority of cars offer safety features which parallel those incorporated in Volvo cars. As such, safety is no longer a core competence, since it has been adopted by the rest of the industry. Thus we can say that a competence which is common throughout an industry is not a core competence for any particular company within that industry unless they are significantly better in it than the competition. For many years, the safety factor in Volvo cars was significantly better than that of other brands; nowadays it is simply on a par with the rest of the industry.

- Thirdly, a core competence should provide a gateway to new markets. This was true in our example of the competing door manufacturers: "entrance technology" opened the gateway to a totally new business area for the company able to divorce a skill from the product in which that skill is embedded. Let us take another example: Sharp has a competence in flat-screen displays, and this competence has given it access to a whole range of markets – lap-top computers, pocket televisions, and video projection screens. Dell may produce excellent computers, yet it is the company's ability to sell these computers by mail order which gives it its competitive edge. Perhaps these edge will eventually be lost as more computer companies enter the mail-order market; when this happens Dell will face the challenge of building a new core competence which will supply it once more with a gateway to new markets.

Searching out the core

At Pieces of Fun, Tom Hoffman was reading his list of capabilities. All the capabilities he had listed were of importance to the company; yet the most important matter, he realized, was to search out the real core of the company. He understood that any core competence must withstand the test of contributing to customer value, of offering a competitor differentiation, and opening a gateway to the future.

Pulling his writing pad to him, he wrote down in capital letters: TECHNOLOGY. Certainly this was one of the aspects of Pieces of Fun which set it apart in the market. Yet looking at the word, Tom thought it was too general. Every company needed technology, and for him this seemed to imply that technology on its own was too broad a term to identify specifically what the company was good at.

Hoffman thought for a while, allowing all aspects of the company's technology to pass a mental review. Occasionally he would jot down a thought on the notepad; then he would cross it out and replace it with another. Finally, however, he seemed satisfied. He nodded and read what he had written: PRINTING AND DIE-CUTTING TECHNOLOGY.

This term, he felt, got to the core of his company's strength. It was, after all, this competence which initially made the company possible. And throughout Pieces of Fun's history, it was the ability to print and die-cut a wide range of materials which had given it the edge over many of the competitors. It was a competence which had made it possible for it to introduce new materials long before its competitors had developed the technology required for using them. It had started printing on cardboard, and later it had moved on to other materials – materials such as wood, plastics, fibers. And each time, it developed high standards of printing and die-cutting which clearly gave it the quality edge. The same determination to allow innovative materials to go hand in hand with the highest qualities of craftsmanship – both in printing and die-cutting – was one of the key factors for the company's continued market leadership.

It was this same philosophy which had allowed the company to move from two-dimensional puzzles to three-dimensional models – something which had caused something of a revolution in what, until then, had been a fairly predictable market.

Hoffman seemed satisfied with this first competence, but he knew there were more. Again he read through the mission statement. This time his eye rested on the opening sentence: *We will provide intellectual entertainment*. Here, he thought, was another competence. The founder, he knew, had always been determined to provide products which not only provided entertainment, but also stimulated the imagination and provided some educational value. Picking up his pen he wrote down: INTELLECTUAL ENTERTAINMENT.

This was an important core competence, he realized, as it was one which had helped the company occupy a unique position in the company's market. The products of Pieces of Fun were perceived as being challenging. They not only provided entertainment, but they also required people to think. To be intellectually challenged. And this, Hoffman knew, had been a contributing factor to the company's reputation and to its competitive edge over its competitors. It was also, he realized, something which was not linked to products – but rather to the inspiration behind those products. This core competence – the ability to entertain, stimulate, and teach at the same time – opened new gateways to the future, since it could be applied to the entertainment market in whatever form the company chose.

Once again his eye went down the list of capabilities. He had a feeling that the historic strength of the company – bedded in the ability to use new materials and techniques – had resulted in another competence. And as he thought, he realized how important graphic design had become over the years. Nodding, he wrote: GRAPHIC DESIGN.

Initially, he knew, the company's strength had been in printing and die-cutting – and this he had already listed as a contributory skill to the first core competence. But he knew that, during the last decade, the introduction of the computer into the design process had resulted in a graphic design competence within the company which not only allowed it to produce excellent designs for traditional products – such as puzzles and board games – but also for computer games. Indeed, the graphic design competence within the company allowed it to move away from two-dimensional design towards three-dimensional design – an essential in the world of computer-based interactive games. It was an important competence which gave Pieces of Fun its leading edge.

Looking through the list of capabilities – which included customer base, market knowledge, logistics, and so on – he realized that the remaining items were all contributory skills, rather than competencies in their own right. Nodding his head he drew a bold line across the sheet of paper; he had, to his own satisfaction, defined the three core competencies which gave Pieces of Fun its uniqueness.

Intellectual entertainment
The ability to design innovative and creative intellectual entertainment

Printing and die-cutting
The ability to print and cut difficult materials in order to produce special games for customers

Graphic design
The ability to develop graphic designs, images, and virtual worlds using desk-top publishing software

Fig 3.2 ■ The three core competencies of Pieces of Fun

The definition process

It would be nice if every process of defining core competencies went as smoothly and as quickly as our example here. But then examples are like that: they move easily and effortlessly through complicated material with an ease which is only found in fiction.

But this book is not about fiction; it is about the hard reality of corporate survival. And for that reason, we have developed a definition process which will, we are convinced, assist you in defining your company's core competencies. The result is a four-step plan, which we will describe here. The full process – with lists and further information – is included in the Value Explorer Toolkit provided with this book. You can use this Toolkit to assist you in defining your core competencies in a detailed way.

Step one: gather together basic information

Before you can start, you have to have certain information about your company, your customers, and your market. These are figures which all managers should have almost at their fingertips, and include such things as turnover, balance position, number of employees, branch, working area, market position, brand and reputation, life-cycle of products and service, and

47

the legal structure, including the ownership of skills and copyrights. Using the lists included in the Value Explorer Toolkit, you can then move through a detailed analysis of your company. By filling in the lists you will be able to:

- define your customers – and the relative importance each customer group has in your present turnover;

- pinpoint shifts in market demands;

- list your major competitors, together with their strengths and weaknesses;

- analyze your company processes, to decide which can continue to be of strategic importance in a changing market;

- analyze your organization and the people you employ;

- list those things which are unique assets to your company – such as brand, quality, reliability, and so on;

- define the skills and capabilities which are of strategic importance within your company;

- list the values and standards which reflect your company;

- define technologies and systems which are essential for continued competitive advantage;

- define leadership and management style – with the courage to be honest about its strengths and weaknesses;

- and finally, list those factors which you are convinced make your company successful.

Step two: creating ideas

Once you have the background information, it is time to allow your creativity to go to work because the facts are one thing; being able to see how all this data fits in with your strategy and your company's strengths and weaknesses requires a lot of careful thought.

One important thing which is often forgotten when attempting to define core competencies is that we shouldn't allow ourselves to be blinded by an internal perspective. Of course we must understand our company and pinpoint those matters which make it unique; but we should never allow ourselves to forget the external perspective. Because ideas can come from anywhere. They can come from a full understanding and appreciation of our products, our intangibles, and the economical engine of our company. But they can equally well come from a better understanding of our customers, about what drives them, what their expectations are, what they want for their lives.

So when we start allowing our creativity to work, we should look at six separate areas.

Look at your customers

Customers are the most valuable asset of your company. They are the ones you have to please. If you are successful, you must already be pleasing them to a large degree. And so you should ask yourself: why do our customers like us? Why do they come to us rather than choose the products or services of one of our competitors? What benefit do we offer to our customers that other companies apparently don't offer?

Next you should ask yourself what advantages you offer your customers. Are they fundamental advantages – ones which set you apart from the rest of the field? And then you should ask yourself which new advantages you would like to offer your customers – and which competencies and skills you will need to acquire in order to offer these advantages successfully and continuously.

The next step is to see how well your ideas about your customers are reflected by your customers themselves. After all, you may *think* you know what they think of you, what they expect of you, why they appreciate you – but do your ideas stand up to a closer scrutiny?

The only way to find out is to ask your customers directly. Preferably in a one-on-one interview situation. You should ask your customers exactly what they think the strong points of your company are. You should ask what they think should be improved. You should ask them what skills they perceive your company possessing. You should ask them where you score better than the competition – and where the competition scores better than you. Make sure the interview is carried out in an open and honest manner. Ask the inter- viewee to be honest. And listen carefully not just to what they say – but also to things they don't say. These are often just as illuminating.

Let us give an example. Suppose you believe that your customers choose you because you offer exceptional quality standards. If none of those interviewed mention quality, it could very well mean that this is less of a decisive factor for them than you had imagined. Perhaps your quality is not so special; perhaps they simply expect high quality from whichever supplier they choose; perhaps they consider it so self-evident that they don't feel the need to mention it; or perhaps they are totally indifferent to the quality which you consider so important, basing their decision to come to you on totally different matters than quality – pricing, perhaps, or delivery reliability, or design. Make sure you listen to questions with an open-mind; this will allow you to hear things which are said – and which are left unspoken!

Look at your products and services
Do your products and services have added value? Be honest! What advantages and benefits do your customers enjoy once they have purchased them or made use of them? Do your products or services add value to your customers and help them enjoy something which they would not otherwise enjoy?

What are the specific requirements you need to manufacture your product or offer your service? Are there any special skills and technologies demanded? Does the product or service require specialized knowledge?

When you are recruiting new employees, is there a specific type of person you need? Do they have to have special knowledge, a specific skill, or a certain mentality? What are the essentials you require them to have in order to do the job properly?

Look at your products and services dispassionately. Try to analyze them from your customers' point of view. Ask yourself a question: it one of your most important stakeholders were to call you and ask you to improve your product or service, what would be the one thing you would try to improve?

Look at your intangibles
We know that there are a lot of intangibles in any company. But do you really know the ones which make the difference in your own. Ask yourself what they are. List them under the five categories already mentioned:

- Skills and tacit knowledge

- Collective values and norms

- Technology and explicit knowledge

- Primary and management processes

- Assets and endowments.

You should also ask yourself which of these intangibles are absolutely essential within your specific branch. There's a good way of determining which of these are of primary importance. Imagine that you have employed a highly skilled professional from a different branch of industry. You have to tell this person those things which are vital within your company. All the pieces of corporate wisdom and technical know-how which everybody in the company needs to know in order to remain successful. What would you tell your new employee? And when you talk about them, which of them could be open to discussion? Which of the gems of wisdom have become folklore and have little or no significance under present circumstances? And which of these ideals could lose their relevance in the future?

Look at your competition

Very few companies enjoy the luxury of being the only supplier in a market. We all face competition. And we should look to our competition to see where we are better than them – and where they are better than us!

First, of course, we have to ask ourselves: who is our current competition? This could very well be different to past competition, or to competition we have always traditionally thought of as competition. For example, as superstores become increasingly prevalent, so traditional department stores will have to consider them as a real competitor – even though in the past they were not operating in markets "owned" by department stores. Similarly, now that gas stations are offering a selection of food products, they can be considered competitors to supermarkets.

A second question you should ask is: who could become competitors in the future? Certainly the examples already given show how volatile markets can be. Is there a threat of new competition arising, say, from emerging technologies, such as Internet?

A very useful exercise is to take a look at the intangibles of your competitors. Using the five categories already mentioned, you should list dispassionately those which make your competitor unique. It requires honesty; but the result will often be very revealing.

A further question you should ask is whether the competition will be able to offer products and services which are the same as yours. If they are lagging behind you – if you are the front-runner in the market – will they be able to catch you up, or even overtake you? If there is the least threat of this, then you should ask yourself how you can improve your existing product or service offering to maintain your competitive edge.

Another useful exercise is to develop a number of strategic scenarios. Let us give some examples:

- List the three most dangerous courses of action your competition could take to win market share from you. Be creative. And be honest. Consider all possibilities – even those which may at present simply seem to belong to the world of fantasy. Then, once you have listed these three strategic threats, plan actions which you could take to thwart them. A further possibility here is, of course, that you come up with ideas which could be of strategic importance to you and give you an even greater lead over your competition!

■ Imagine that you were offered the job of CEO by your leading competitor. What actions would you take in your new job to attack your previous (i.e. your present) company? Such a scenario helps expose strategic weaknesses in your present company and can help you devise improvement programs to rectify the situation before you come under attack.

■ Make a list of fundamental factors which distinguish your market's winners from the losers. Again be honest with yourself and look at your company's present position. Draw up plans to eliminate the losing factors and increase the winning factors.

And finally, ask yourself how you plan to cope with the competition in the broadest sense of the word. Look at your answers and see whether you have exposed your competitors' Achilles heels. Know what you are attacking – and develop plans which make the most of your strengths – and the most of your competitors' weaknesses.

Look at successful projects or product innovations
What makes a product a success? Is it because of technology? Customer appeal? Added benefits? Analyze successful products and services and find out what has given them their success.

Look at the successes in your company's past. What contributed to that success? What aspects need to be continued into the future – and what aspects need to be relegated to the past. Richard D'Aveni, professor of Strategic Management at the Amos Tuck School of Business Administration, Dartmouth College, says: "We mustn't learn how to remember, we must learn how to forget."[3] He believes that many companies get stuck in the successes of the past, rather than addressing the challenges of the future. Are you guilty of this? And does this attachment to the past have adverse effects on the way you address the future?

List recent landmarks in your company's success story. Ask yourself what factors have contributed to these successes. Are they due to the development of a new technology? The creative use of an existing skill? Were they the result of an acquisition? Or because you recently increased your pool of talented employees? It is vital to identify the source of success and see whether the same source can produce new successes in the future. Or whether you need to look elsewhere for new success.

Look at your present innovations. What new products and services are in the pipeline? Are they totally new developments – or are they a reaction to the success of a competitor? Do these imminent innovations add value to your company and to the way your customers benefit from using your products or services?

Look at your future

Markets change with increasing rapidity. Here today and gone tomorrow is the norm rather than the exception. Many experts maintain that there is no way of knowing the future; we must learn to navigate in a world in constant change.

Yet it is vital for any manager to envisage the future. Perhaps that vision may never occur; the process of envisaging it can be very valuable indeed for you as a manager.

Scenarios play an important role here. Let us suggest two exercises:

- Imagine that in the coming ten years your company's prospects became so bad that there is only a 10% chance that things could get any worse. You have almost hit rock bottom. Can you describe that future? Can you list internal and external causes for such a doomsday scenario? Be honest. Look failure in the face and describe the causes of that failure.

- Imagine that in the coming ten years your company's prospects improve to such a degree that there is only a 10% chance that things will improve even further. Can you describe that future? Can you list all the external causes and internal measures which will have created such a rosy future? Again be honest. Look success in the face and describe the reasons for that success.

Step three: define a number of preliminary core competencies

You've completed all the preparatory work. You have now a better view of your company than you have ever had before. You know all the forces working in your market – customers, innovation, competition. You have listed intangibles which you believe are essential for success. You know where you stand in comparison to your main competitors.

Now is the time to define a number of preliminary core competencies. Preliminary?

Yes. Because at the moment we are suggesting that you look at a variety of options open to you and list them in core competencies. We are moving from a list of capabilities to those competencies which are vital for your continued success. And at a later stage, after we have taken a look at the strengths and weaknesses of the core competencies, we will probably need to refine the list even more as we try to help you reach to the very heart of your company.

We have seen how Tom Hoffman defined the core competencies of Pieces of Fun, analyzing the skills and capabilities required for continued success. We would suggest a number of steps:

- Start with "the ability to ..." For Hoffman, this was the ability to use technology, in particular printing and die-cutting technology. Your company may have a unique ability to do something which sets you apart from the rest of the competition. Try to define this uniqueness.

- Think of a combination of skills, knowledge, processes, and culture which together form a unique competence. Hoffman saw how various capabilities resulted in a competence to offer intellectual entertainment. This was clearly a combination of a whole range of skills and capabilities.

- Always think of a customer benefit. You work for your customer, and a core competence should always reflect a benefit for your customer. Intellectual entertainment was obviously such a customer benefit.

- If you can, give your core competence a catchy name. Again, intellectual entertainment is a good description of the competence and is more easily remembered than a longer description such as "the ability to offer entertainment in the broadest sense of the word which is at the same time stimulating and mentally challenging."

- Write down a very precise description of the core competence. The uniqueness of your company is probably founded in very subtle things. Catching this subtlety in a definition is the most important step in deter-mining your core competencies. If you fail to do so, your competencies will be experienced by others as platitudes, cliches or trivialities that are applicable to any other company. To force yourself to be very precise you should provide definitions and synonyms for every important word in your core competence description.

Step four: break down your competencies into intangibles

As we have already seen, each competence will be the result of a number of intangibles. It is right now to see which intangibles contribute to the specific competence. In this way, specific areas which need attention can be isolated and strategic solutions can be designed to address each of the issues individually. This is a far easier strategy than trying to address a competence in its totality.

Walt Disney is an enterprise with an extremely wide variety of activities. Yet, no matter which activity is developed, it always revolves around a single core competence: family entertainment. Yet not just any entertainment will do: whatever the company undertakes must be entirely original, perfectly executed, and created to delight a wide audience. The result of concentrating on family entertainment has resulted not only in films and video productions, but also theme parks, hotels, video-by-cable distribution, and film studios.[4]

The core competence is the result of a variety of intangibles. The primary management processes at Disney is directed at generating as much income as possible from each new project. Even when a film is still on the drawing-board, management already actively discusses merchandising deals, granting rights to companies that will create marketing to fuel Disney's sales.[5] In marketing, the tight distribution system created by Walt Disney allows for a constant remarketing of products time and again. In this way, films enjoy an absolute deluge of new marketing possibilities, from domestic and international home videos and network and foreign television runs to pay-per-view and cable offerings. Next, a film will generate new theme park rides and characters, new products in Disney stores (toys, clothing, books, games, records, CD-ROMs), new television spin-offs, and programming ideas for Disney's radio networks. Animated features become live-action films and Broadway shows. Cross-pollination of a single idea throughout every single department that could somehow make use of that idea is a key factor in Disney's success.[6] Nothing at Disney is left to chance. Even the creative process is a well-planned process. A rigid nine-step regime for project management was created through which Disney exercises tight control on the creative process, allowing long-term vision to be aligned with short-term execution. This allows cost cuts and speedy production.[7]

But management guidelines are not the only weapon at Disney. There are two additional structures which ensure that everybody is involved in "creating the magic." The first is a structure which dates back to the 1950s: the so-called Imagineering group of creative talent. Here, more than 2,000 creative specialists spend their time dreaming up ever more sophisticated thrills for the Disney product. A special feature is the Dream retreats, in which the Imagineers are propelled into a world of new ideas and give the employees a chance to dream and express their creativity. These retreats not only stimulate personal creative satisfaction, but also encourage commitment to the company. What's more, they open up a vast new resource of knowledge and innovative ideas from which the company can draw. A second structure for harvesting ideas is the Gong Shows, held three times a year, in which anyone who thinks he or she has a good idea can formally take a pitch to a panel of top executives including the CEO. These shows help employees understand why some ideas work – and why others don't.[8]

But there is also something else which supports the Disney image: the collective value and norms which are summed up in the management philosophy: Dream, Believe, Dare, Do. Walt Disney had a passionate belief in the need for a strong corporate culture and to this end he instigated a formal training program that has become known as the Disney University. Today every new employee – at whatever level in the company – is required to attend training which not only concentrates on the skills needed for specific tasks, but also on ensuring that the new employee has a full understanding of the company's culture and traditions. Such is the success of the training devised by Disney – and it includes on-job training and aims at giving employees guidelines, rather than strict dictates, so that they are encouraged to exercise good judgement – that it is now marketed to other companies.[9]

This example shows how a core competence is the result of a variety of intangibles, including assets and endowments, primary management processes, skills and tacit knowledge, collective value and norms, and technology and explicit knowledge. Let us now see how Tom Hoffman of Pieces of Fun breaks down his three core competencies into their contributing intangibles.

⊔ Contributing elements

Hoffman seemed pleased with his list of core competencies. But he knew that each such competence was the result of a wide range of intangible elements within his company. To gain true insight into all the forces at play within the company, he decided to try to list these elements to achieve a true helicopter view for himself.

Again pulling the notepad towards him, he started noting the various elements which contributed to the first core competence "Printing and Die-cutting." When he was finished, he catalogued them into groups. Those very groups which we discussed in the first chapter.

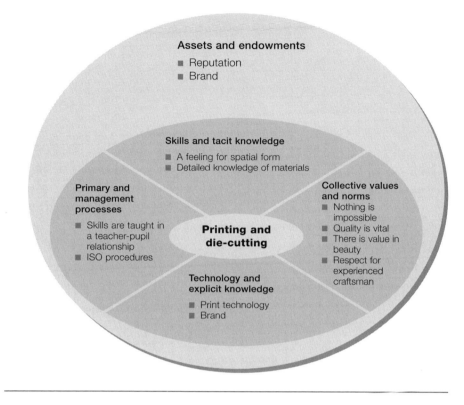

Fig 3.3 ■ Printing and die-cutting core competence broken down into intangibles

Skills and tacit knowledge

■ *A feeling for spatial form*. This was the very heart of everything they did. A puzzle or game always existed in space, in form. Understanding how this space or form could be so constructed that it resulted in a fascinating and challenging game for people of all ages was key to a product's success. It was also key to the way that product was designed and produced.

■ *Understanding what is possible and what is not*. This, he knew, was vital to successfully introducing new products. This understanding was important not only for those in production, but also for those in development. Although he always urged his developers to "chase the impossible dream," he also made it clear that even those dreams had eventually to be turned into reality. Stretching the limits of the company was acceptable, even essential; but they must never be stretched to breaking point. He also realized that this understanding was something shared by many people within the company. In fact, it was essential that it be shared. Each new product was the result of the work of a whole range of people within the company, and each of them had to have this understanding of what was possible and what was impossible within their own specific competence area.

■ *The technical knowledge and ability to prevent breakdowns and correct them efficiently if they should happen.* The company depended on its reputation for high standards and top quality, but also on its ability to meet deadlines and supply products to its clients on time. For this, the company depended very heavily on a production process which was as reliable as possible. Quality assurance was just as, if not more, important than quality control. And ensuring that processes were carefully geared to each other and the demands on each part of the process were understood. In this way, potentially disruptive breakdowns were virtually eliminated from the total production process.

■ *Detailed knowledge of materials.* All the skills of the printer – the knowledge of inks, of paper, cardboard, plastics – were essential to the quality of the total process. Similarly, knowledge of the properties of the materials had played an important role in the company achieving its recognized position in the field of die-cutting. Such skills were all part of the craftsmanship which the company considered of essential importance for the success of its products. In addition, they contributed to the company's lead in the fields of innovative and high quality products. As such, this knowledge had to be nurtured and constantly maintained up to date.

Collective values and norms

■ *Nothing is impossible.* The company had proved in the past how it was wrong to assume that something couldn't be done. When it had started thinking about printing on wood and plastic, specialists had told them it would be impossible. It proved the contrary. And this had instilled in everybody in the company the belief that they could do anything. Or at least try to do it. Nothing was ever dismissed out of hand; people were encouraged to think out of the box.

■ *Quality is vital.* It was this aspect which had played a major role in Pieces of Fun achieving its leading position in the market-place. And it was quality in the broadest sense of the word. Quality in printing, die-cutting, and production. Quality in customer relations and logistics. Quality, too, in content, in entertainment, in innovation, in excitement. And, Hoffman realizes, this constant focus on quality was essential in the future. After all, which market leader was *not* quality conscious?

■ *There is value in beauty*. Throughout its history, Pieces of Fun had paid particular attention to the aesthetic value of its products. From innovation, through design, to printing, die-cutting, manufacture, and packaging, the artistic qualities of the product were always of enormous importance. An awareness for this aesthetic side of the business had become a way of life for everybody in the company. Hoffman – and with him, he believed, his clients – would have it no other way.

■ *Respect for experienced craftsman*. It is always tempting, Hoffman knew, to prepare for the future by throwing away the past. Certainly a company must never be inhibited by the past; but nor should it disregard the experience of craftsman who have shown an ability to think ahead, to create new applications using their knowledge of their craft.

Technology and explicit knowledge

■ *Print technology*. This had always been a key element for the success of the company. Yet it was the ability to adapt to new challenges – first by printing on wood, then on plastic, and later on other materials – while still retaining an unparalleled quality which had contributed so much to the present skills in the company.

■ *Die-cutting technology*. This, again, was a technology which was a key factor for the company. But once again – in common with the print technology – it had adapted to new challenges of materials. This had resulted in a die-cutting technology which was recognized as second to none in the industry.

Primary and management processes

■ *Skills are taught in a teacher-pupil relationship*. The old idea of apprenticeships is still in use at Pieces of Fun. Experienced craftsman are encouraged to share their knowledge with their younger colleagues. In this way, the experience within the company is retained for the next generation.

■ *ISO procedures*. Pieces of Fun had decided early to ensure that their production and logistics processes met the very highest standards. And for this reason, a concerted effort by everybody within the company had resulted in it gaining an ISO certificate. What's more, the ISO procedures which had been put in place were adhered to at all times, ensuring that everybody understood the various processes and way they interlocked to achieve a seamless process flow within the organization.

Assets and endowments

■ *Reputation.* This was something of which everybody within Pieces of Fun was proud. It had been achieved thanks to a common vision and a non-stop determination to be the best. The company's acceptance within the trade and its ability to produce high quality products with a true entertainment and educational content had resulted in a reputation which contributed enormously to the company's sales. But this was only part of its reputation: the other was the way it serviced its clients; its commitment to deadlines; its knowledge of the market which resulted in new products to meet the changing demands of the customers. Hoffman knew that a reputation took a long time to build – but could be destroyed overnight.

■ *Brand.* The quality brand image had again been achieved over a long period of time. It was developing all the time in line with the changing market. A strong brand was essential if the company was to achieve success in new markets and new segments. It was closely allied to the reputation which they enjoyed.

Hoffman nodded again. He certainly had a better feeling for the direction his strategy should take now he knew the contribution each of the intangibles made to the core competence. And he saw that having a picture of each contributing asset allowed him to take measures which he may otherwise have overlooked. Pulling the paper to him, he proceeded to list the intangibles for the other two core competencies.

⌐ Defining core competencies at various levels of abstraction

So you now have your list of provisional core competencies and, hopefully, you have, like Tom Hoffman, decided which intangibles make a contribution to each competence.

Pieces of Fun, however, is a smallish company, with a fairly prescribed market area. It is not particularly diversified – although such diversification may become necessary in the future as the games and entertainment markets make new demands on suppliers and game developers – so the three core competencies of our example are applicable to the company as a whole. This is, however, not always the case. Many companies operate in a range of markets, each with their own specific parameters and demands, which make it very difficult indeed to define a core competence which is applicable to all areas of such a company's activities. In such cases, it is essential to decide which competence is applicable to which market area.

If you are in such a diversified situation, then perhaps the best way to start your competence definition process is at a product or business unit level. You may discover that each business unit has its own competence. Do not consider this diversity as a sign of weakness; rather accept it as a result of the business you are in. Later, when you have developed competencies for each of the various sections of your company you can use these to find similarities which can then form the heart of a company-wide core competence. On the other hand, your business may be so diverse that this will prove impossible. In that case, don't worry. Many companies exist with clusters of competencies, each contributing to a specific market segment.

Let us give an example. The Canadian telecommunications giant Northern Telecom (Nortel) announced that it has concluded tests on providing consumers access to internet via their electricity cables. It had developed this technology together with Norweb Communications, which has had experience in telephony via electricity cables. The question posed by this development is whether the electricity generators now need to develop a telecommunications competence or whether joint ventures will become the order of the day. Whichever route is chosen, it is obvious that each section will need separate competencies. We are likely to see this trend continue as a further integration of infrastructural facilities occur.

Levels of competencies

Another tool to help you move through the various competencies you may have described for your company is to consider each at a different level of abstraction. We define four levels of abstraction:

- *Individual competencies* – those required by individuals working in the company;
- *Team competencies* – those required and shared by a number of people working in a department or on a project;
- *Core competencies* – those competencies required by a business unit in a large organization or by a dedicated company;
- *Mega competencies* – those which conjure up an association in people's minds when they are exposed to a brand, e.g. Pepsi, McDonald's, or Nike.

⊔ Leverage your knowledge

Defining core competencies and the intangibles associated with each competence is a remarkably revealing exercise. It gives you a fuller understanding of the forces operating within your company. It can help you isolate areas which need greater attention. It can show where your company needs to strengthen itself. It gives insight into new potentials for the existing capabilities within your company. It can tell you what must be nurtured and what has outlived its usefulness.

But most importantly, it will enable you to understand the potential within your company – the potential of intangibles – which can help you leverage your knowledge into something which adds value to your company, your product and service, and your customer. Something which ultimately will have a positive effect on your market value. In the next chapter we make a start by helping you to assess your strengths.

4

T om Hoffman looked at his analysis of his company's core competencies and seemed satisfied. But as he sat alone in his office, he
wondered how he could put his analysis to practical use. He had the feeling that
he had the building bricks in his hand; all he now needed to do, he thought, was
find of way of using these bricks to build his company of tomorrow. He now knew
the important competencies within his company. His question now was: how did
they help him create sustainability for the future?

He knew that there was an incredible turbulence in the US toy market. It is
a very lucrative market, worth something like $22 billion a year. Not surprisingly, it
had attracted a large number of competitors, all interested in gaining a slice of a
very tasty pie. This had resulted in a constant shift in attention given to certain
aspects of the market by its leading players. Mattel, the market leader with net
sales of $5.5 billion in 1999, had realized that, with the increasing growth of inter-
active entertainment, it would need to strengthen its software capabilities. This it
did by merging with The Learning Company, thus creating net sales in software of
more than $1 billion. Hasbro, the world number two, with world-wide net revenues
of $4.2 billion in 1999, similarly made important acquisitions of software
companies, by taking over the software game specialist MicroProse Inc. and Tiger
Electronics, the manufacturer of Furby. All this, Tom Hoffman acknowledged,
showed how the market was shifting away from the traditional game area of
puzzles and board games towards electronic games.

How, he asked himself, would the core competencies he had listed for
Pieces of Fun help them maintain a profitable position in this changing market?

But there was more change taking place in his market. The toy market was traditionally a market for children. But, as the *New York Times* reported in 1998,[1] "Kids are not buying toys the way they used to. They are graduating out of toys at a younger age."

This shift was worrying for many toy manufacturers; for Hoffman, however, it was less of a threat than it at first seemed. His analysis had clearly shown that Pieces of Fun was not in the business of toys, but of "intellectual entertainment." This implied that its products were aimed at an adult public. But he also knew that today's adults were yesterday's children. He couldn't afford to ignore such an important group as kids, when they would grow up to become his prime target audience.

With all these considerations in mind, Tom asked himself how his company's core competencies would hold up in this changing market. Were they strong enough in the new situation? Were they under attack? Were they sufficient to give his company sustainability? Could they help ward off competition?

⊐ Core competencies: theory or practice?

The question facing Tom Hoffman faces every managing director. How do today's core competencies – often built up over a long period and representing a considerable investment in time, money, people, and skills – equip your company for competitive success in a changing market?

> How do today's core competencies equip your company for competitive success in a changing market?

When discussing core competencies, traditional literature maintains that unless a suggested core competence meets all the criteria laid down for it, it should not be considered as such. While this is fine in theory, it does not always work in practice. In extreme cases, an analysis along "traditional" theoretical lines may show that a company has no core competencies at all! And this is something we would oppose very strongly. For theory and practice are two entirely different things – which is why we want to make this book as practical as possible!

For many companies – and this may very well include yours – a company competence may qualify as a core competence, even if it does not meet all criteria laid down. In our view, the *strength* of each of the competencies which you have defined is of far greater relevance than the name we give to them.

Such strength is not consistent. It varies. A competence may be very strong in one area, but weaker in another. For managers, it is important to be able to assess the varying strengths of the competencies they have defined. And for this reason, we have drawn up a list of criteria which will help you to determine the *practical* strength of each competence within your own market area.

Five criteria for evaluating the strength of a core competence

Of little value		Of great value
No value added to the customer	**Added-value test**	Clearly value added to the customer
Poorer or equal to the competition	**Competitiveness test**	Better than the competition
Soon to be commonplace	**Potentiality test**	Creates new opportunities
Easy to imitate	**Sustainability test**	Difficult to imitate
Vulnerable	**Robustness test**	Securely anchored in the organization

Fig. 4.1 ■ Five criteria for evaluating the strength of a core competence

We believe that the strength of a core competence depends on the following five criteria:

■ **It should add value for customers**. You must ask yourself whether the core competence you are analyzing creates a substantial benefit for your customer or whether it provides your company with a substantial cost benefit. This is a vital point, since we are now entering a new economy where, according to Kevin Kelly,[2] you need to add more value at less cost. In their book *Competing for the Future*,[3] Hamel and Prahalad call this "Customer Value."

■ **It should give you a competitive edge**. You must ask yourself whether you are better in this specific competence than your competitors. Does it make you unique? As we have already seen, a competence which is shared by every company in an industry is little more than a skill, unless one company is significantly better in it than other companies. Hamel and Prahalad call this "Competitor Differentiation."[4]

■ **It should offer potential for the future**. The life-cycle of products is decreasing all the time. Only a decade ago, the life-cycle of a PC was calculated in years; now it is frequently calculated in months. For companies this means that you must get your products to the market quicker than ever before. John Cleese, the British comedian of *Monty Python* fame, recently said: "We've spent the last thirty years developing an incredible number of labor-saving appliances – and the result is we have less time than ever before." In business, we are, quite simply, living in a time when there is never enough time! Cor Boonstra, CEO of Royal Philips put it another way: "We are living in Internet years – and there, a year lasts just one month!" Your competencies must be able to feed innovation, so that you can beat your competitors to the market-place. They must provide the gateway to the markets of tomorrow. Hamel and Prahalad[5] call this "Extendibility."

■ **It should be sustainable for several years**. You must ask yourself whether the competence can enable you to stay ahead of the competition for a substantial period of time. Or will it be something which the competition will be able to pick up quite simply, thus destroying your advantage?

■ **It should be firmly anchored in your organization**. It is little use having a competence which is shared by just a tiny group of individuals; they could leave and take the competence with them. This was brought home very clearly to ING Barings Bank, when half of their very successful Taiwanese team, which had achieved record trading on the growing Taiwanese stock exchange, deflected to Merrill Lynch.[6] A core competence must be rooted in the organization, shared by the majority of people within that organization. But we should place a word of warning here: you should beware of core rigidities. "We've always done it that way" should not mean "that is the only way we are prepared to do it."

⌑ How strong is Pieces of Fun?

Tom Hoffman looked at his list of competencies and decided to apply the five-point criteria test to them to see exactly how strong each of them really was. He started with *Added Value*.

The question he needed to ask himself was: does the core competence create a substantial benefit for the customer or does it provide Pieces of Fun with a substantial cost benefit?

As he looked down the list of competencies, he thought that each of them did add value for the customer. The "Printing and die-cutting" allowed the company to produce unique, differentiated 2D and 3D puzzles. These still appealed to a large number of customers, who had come to appreciate the high level of quality and finish which had become synonymous with a Pieces of Fun product. In fact, Tom was proud that many of his company's products had achieved "classic" status. They were often collector's items, fetching high prices at auctions and sales. He thought that they would continue to be in demand, although he realized that this would never be more than a small, niche market. But the finishing quality, he also realized, was not the core of the matter; rather it made the products made by Pieces of Fun "nice to have."

More fundamental to customer added value were "Graphic design" and "Intellectual entertainment." These added considerable value to the products of Pieces of Fun; in fact, he knew from market research that these were often the qualities which attracted his customers in the first place.

Testing for added value

The analysis described here gives a very good idea of how each core competence can make its own contribution to the perceived added value for the customer. To assist you with your analysis, we have developed a checklist for each of the five criteria. Each of these checklists provides a series of questions which should be addressed when judging the competencies in combination. On the Added Value checklist, we have identified the following five important areas which you should consider.

- The core competence offers a substantial benefit for your customers or a substantial cost-saving for your company.
- Customers demand this specific benefit or cost-saving.
- This benefit is important for a large number of customers; it goes further than just "nice to have."
- Customers will continue expecting this benefit for the foreseeable future; it is not simply a passing fancy.
- Leadership in this core competence makes customers think you are different to the competition, rather than just better.

The input for answering these questions can come from a variety of sources.

But what you always have to remember is that you should be able to judge the extent to which the customer appreciates the benefits or cost-savings resulting from the core competence. Many companies use customer satisfaction surveys for this; some use it for input, others as a litmus test for their own findings.

When Toyota introduced its Lexus, it entered a segment which, until then, had been dominated by Mercedes. A Mercedes owner traditionally appreciated the high quality of the German car – because of both the technical superiority of Mercedes and the lack of defects for which the car was famous. Obviously such high quality came at a premium, but buyers were quite prepared to pay the extra price for the car. Mercedes achieved this high level of quality by using skilled craftsman who "hand made" the car. But this had a negative side-effect for the company: a third of Mercedes' production capacity was involved in tracking down and eliminating faults which had occurred in the assembly process – the same amount that Toyota used to produce a car without defects in one go! The customer, however, was unaware of all the efforts made by Mercedes to produce the perfect car, and this, therefore, had little or no added value for the buyer. Toyota was able to achieve the same perceived high level of quality at a much lower price, which proved clearly advantageous in the market-place.[7] The ability to produce defect-free cars for a lower price was rewarded by a growing share of the luxury car segment.

The "Battle of the VCRs" is another example of how customers look at things differently to manufacturers. Three companies had entered the market with their own video systems: Philips, with its V2000 system, Sony, with its Betamax system, and JVC, with its VHS system. Experts agree that the VHS system was the inferior in terms of technical performance. But JVC adopted a strategy of broad licensing agreements with a large number of manufacturers. This resulted in a far better distribution network and a greater variety of VHS models for the customer. The greater availability of VHS hardware had a further impact on the available software: film companies saw greater market opportunities from producing VHS versions of their products, rather than V2000 or Betamax. The result was that the customer had a wider variety of choice of pre-recorded videotapes for the VHS system than for either of the others. This only strengthened the market position of JVC. Ultimately, both Philips and Sony withdrew their systems from this market, even though they were technically superior.[8] A Philips director responsible for the company's VCR policy later made headline news by stating that the Philips system had failed because there was hardly any pornography available on V2000 pre-recorded tapes! All this shows that while Philips and Sony both believed that high technical quality would win the day, customers preferred greater choice, both in hardware and software, and were willing to sacrifice quality to that choice. A similar war has taken place between the Philips DCC cassette based audio recording system and Sony's MiniDisc. Although the sound reproduction of the DCC was superior to that of the MiniDisc, consumers decided that other benefits were more important, such as instant access to individual tracks which they had come to expect from the CD.

Honda, the Japanese automotive manufacturer, prides itself on its skills and knowledge to design and build small, reliable, and smooth-running engines and power-trains. But this, for the consumer, is not enough. In today's technological world, consumers have come to expect cars which run well. It is the market perception that there are "no bad cars." Technology, like safety, has become something which the market takes as a matter-of-course; buying decisions are based on a whole range of other aspects. And this is where the true strength of Honda lies. It has, over the years, developed and implemented a whole range of business processes which the consumer feels "adds value" to purchasing a Honda car. Honda has invested considerably in a high-quality dealer network, backing this up with an extensive training and support program. The dealers' merchandising, selling, floor planning, and service management are consciously aimed at providing a high level of service at all stages in the buying and owning process.[9] Honda dealers make a point of showing customers their modern, super-clean workshops and stress the special collecting and delivering service offered to customers when repair or service is required.

⌐ How competitive is Pieces of Fun?

This was a question which caused Tom Hoffman a lot of thought. Was Pieces of Fun competitive? Certainly it was not the only company producing intellectual games. Nor was it likely to become that in the near future. It was faced, liked everybody else in every market, with competitors. Some very good. Others less good. But all wanted a share of the market. All were determined to make a profit. Certainly he knew Pieces of Fun could still enjoy a strong reputation for the intellectual content of its puzzles. He knew many enthusiasts still found its products challenging in the best possible way. But was this enough to remain ahead of the competition?

Tom frowned slightly and once again read down the list of competencies, weighing their competitive advantage in his mind. Perhaps he would find the answer here.

He thought about his company's printing and die-cutting technology. He liked to think they were still ahead of the field in this area, but he knew that other companies were rapidly closing the gap. Fink and Son, for example, was already offering products at a level which approached that of his own company. In fact, Fink and Son had recently introduced a series of "crafted" puzzles, which in some cases were almost as good as his own company's games. He doubted whether this competence gave him any true competitive advantage, since others in the market were matching if not surpassing him in this field.

He also frowned when he thought about the graphic design competence. He knew his company produced top-class designs, but so did a lot of other companies. What's more, graphic design was becoming common property, what with the emergence of computer programs and desk-top publishing which allowed even the most inexperienced designer to produce something special. There was little competitive advantage there, he admitted.

He reached for his checklist and started filling in his score.

Testing for competitiveness

No company has a market all to itself. Indeed, if this threatens to happen, many governments start anti-trust suits aimed at providing the opportunity for competition. Microsoft has lived with such a threat for some time. Similarly, many traditionally public services – such as electricity, gas, and postal services – which were traditionally a state-owned monopoly are now being privatized to ensure competition and thus, the argument goes, promote better deals for the consumer.

So how can we use our core competencies to decide our competitiveness? There are again five questions we have to ask ourselves for each of our competencies.

- Do fewer than five of our competitors share this particular competence?

- Are we superior to our competitors in most aspects of a particular competence?

- Do we invest substantially more time and energy in a particular competence than our competitors?

- Do our customers choose our products because they perceive our expertise in this particular competence as something important or desirable?

- Can we prove our leadership and superiority in this particular competence, for example with articles in trade magazines or patents and so on?

Many companies find market research, customer satisfaction surveys, and so on particularly valuable in helping them determine the competitive strength of their competencies.

Intel is a company which has built up a strong corporate image in the highly competitive world of memories and processors. Its marketing capacity is strongly dependent on this corporate image, and so, in its marketing efforts, the company does everything possible to make use of its strong corporate identity.[10]

Some international companies enjoy a strong competence in a specific area, and it is vital that this competence is then recognized within the structure of the company. At Procter & Gamble, for example, there is a world-class marketing competence. This, however, is located in what many companies would call the advertising department, but which at Procter & Gamble is called "Brand Management." [11]

Many companies have found that a strongly developed competence in after-sales service can be of considerable competitive advantage. Caterpillar, for example, the manufacturer of heavy ground-moving equipment for the construction industry, has developed an after-sales service which guarantees that any spare part can be delivered to any location in the world within 24 hours. Such a service has proved of great competitive value to Caterpillar and is largely responsible for its present level of success.[12]

One of the most spectacular competitive successes of recent years was the ability of Wal-Mart to overtake the world leader Kmart in just ten years. Today, Wal-Mart is the world's largest and most profitable retail organization. How could this happen in such a short time?

When Wal-Mart launched its attack on the position of Kmart, it defined a simple mission: customers had to be able to buy high-quality products, at a time and a place which suited them. In addition, Wal-Mart had to offer a highly competitive costing structure and build up a strong and lasting reputation in the field of reliability.

It was a tall order, yet Wal-Mart approached it by including supply chain management in its competitive strategy. It developed a number of support systems which demanded very high investments – so high, in fact, that they seemed to fly in the face of current common-sense investment strategy. Yet the result was a permanently low cost-level and an important acquisition of knowledge in supply management, which has contributed considerably to its present strong reputation.

A similar story of very high investments is at the core of the success of Ikea, the Swedish chain of furniture and interior design department stores.

The investments were not only in the department stores themselves, but also in distribution centers, in purchasing departments throughout the world, and in technical and financial help to suppliers. The result of these investments is an economy of scale which allows Ikea to maintain an almost unassailable position as high quality, low cost full-range interior store throughout the world. It is the system which Ikea has developed over the years which is now one of its strongest competitive competencies.

If we look at these examples, then we see that the core competitive competence was often something which may not appear important without a deeper knowledge of the company. For Wal-Mart and Ikea, it was not simply the range of products or the low prices which were responsible for their competitive success; in both cases it was the carefully developed business processes – and mainly that of supply chain management – which gives the companies the ability to operate in the successful way they do. For Intel it was not just the quality of their memories and chips; rather it was the strong corporate reputation which was of major importance for the success.

All this shows clearly that when we investigate our own company for its competitiveness, we should look beyond the obvious. Sometimes the importance of a core competence for our competitiveness may be un-expectedly large; conversely, what we thought was the main competence for our competitiveness may be of less importance than we had been led to believe. An open-mind here – and the desire to look further than the obvious – are key factors for a successful analysis.

⌐ What is the potential of Pieces of Fun?

Tom Hoffman pulled the next checklist towards him across the desk. He was fully aware that success in his branch meant the ability to come up with new concepts at an ever-increasing regularity. Did his company's core competencies give him the tools and abilities he needed to develop a whole new range of intellectually challenging games?

He once again looked through his list of core competencies. He immedi-ately disregarded the Printing and die-cutting technology; it was a competence which was an inheritance of the past, but gave little advantage in the future. The world of games was changing, and Tom, if he were honest with himself, would have to agree that the days of traditional puzzles were numbered. He knew that this competence would only allow him the expand further with 2D and 3D puzzles – but the market for those, he knew, was shrinking. Not much potential there he thought.

But he was not completely disheartened, because he realized that two of his other core competencies – Graphic design and Intellectual entertainment – offered greater potential. Multimedia and the internet had provided graphic designers with a whole new playing-field – larger than anything ever known in the past. The possibilities for design and graphic manipulation of images were virtually limitless, and a strong competence in this field offered enormous potential for the future. And the same applied, he thought, to Intellectual Entertainment: people wanted to be challenged – and this had been a main contributor to the success of Pieces of Fun in the past – and he was convinced that even in a new age of play, intellectual entertainment would remain a key factor in determining the success of a new game.

Testing for potential

The key question we have to ask ourselves when examining our core competencies for potential is whether the specific competence can provide an answer to a demand which is increasing – or which is expected to increase in the future – and whether it allows us to create new products and services. In addition, we should address other matters – such as market and social trends – which could threaten our ability to use a core competence.

Our checklist again lists five questions which should be considered when deciding the potential of a core competence:

- Is there an increasing demand for products and services which can be satisfied thanks to this specific core competence?
- Does the core competence provide us with the ability to create new products and services in the future?
- Does the core competence give us the ability to expand into new markets, or service markets which may develop in the future?
- Are we sure there are no economic threats – whether from customers, suppliers, or competitors – which could adversely affect our application of the competence?
- Are we sure there are no social threats – whether from pressure groups, legislation, or changing social attitudes – which could adversely affect our application of the competence?

Tools which you could find useful in this area are close analyses of the life-cycles of past products to which a core competence made a specific contribution, and projecting the findings into the future. An S-curve analysis –

which charts the growth and inevitable decline of a specific product or service – can show where new products or services will need to be introduced in order to offset the inevitable decline of existing products. Again, this can be projected onto each core competence, to see how far it is able to contribute in the next generation of products, services, and markets.

Japan Tobacco, the country's partly privatized monopoly producer of cigarettes, has clearly determined that the demand for cigarettes will decline from 2005 onward. In order to redress the balance, other areas will need to be encouraged if the company is to continue to be successful in the face of declining demand for its key product. The direction in which the company is now moving was first suggested by the enormous success of peach-flavored mineral water, introduced by one of the company's food divisions. This has encouraged the company to move more determinedly into the food market, and it has now built an organic-vegetable business and has acquired a chain of Italian restaurants. The company's aim is to double sales from non-tobacco products to 100 million yen by the year 2005. Japan Tobacco says that a tobacco company must place itself in a position to solve the effects of a decreasing market.[13]

> The key question when examining competencies for potential is whether the specific competence can provide an answer to a demand which is increasing.

The actions being contemplated by Sara Lee – not only one of the world's largest food and cake supplier, but also the company which owns some of the world's best-known brands such as Wonderbra, Champion sportswear, and Hanes underwear – are nothing short of drastic: it is now planning to withdraw totally from the manufacture of clothing, deciding, instead, to follow the example of Nike and only attach its brand-name to products produced by external suppliers. It is even contemplating selling its food business.[14]

We have already mentioned the success of Ikea, the Swedish company which has built up a world-wide reputation for high-quality, low-price furniture and interior design articles. It would be perfectly feasible for Ikea to make use of its existing brand values and move them into new market areas. In fact, the company had actually investigated the possibility of moving into the hotel business, by opening a chain of hotels which would offer good quality accommodation for a low price. The plan, however, was shelved when Ikea was unable to find a suitable partner for this venture.[15]

Another Swedish company – this time the insurance and banking giant, Skandia – has been paying a lot of attention to the whole area of intellectual capital and what this means for the company and its financial statements. At the moment Leif Edvinsson, the company's director of intellectual capital, is leading a team of 30 people, which is investigating five specific areas of the company's business: the European insurance market, demographics, technology, the world economy, and organization and leadership. Using this input, the team hopes to develop a vision of the future, which will be presented to the company's 150 senior executives.[16]

What these examples illustrate is that even successful companies have to reassess their businesses on a regular basis in order to decide where the most potential can be found. Using the potential checklist to analyze your core competencies can provide you with invaluable information which can help you design a successful future for your company.

◩ How sustainable is Pieces of Fun?

Tom pulled the next checklist towards him and looked at the title: Sustainability. He thought about this for a moment, a slight crease in his forehead showing his concentration. But then he smiled and nodded to himself. He knew that some of his company's core competencies placed him in a good position for the present, offered some chance of competitiveness, and gave the company some potential for the future. But he realized that in order to be successful in the long term, the core competencies would need to be sustainable.

Looking down the list, the frown returned to his face once more. His company may be doing fairly well at the moment – but what about next year? He had to be honest and say that none of the core competencies were so unique that they could not be copied by the competitors. What's more, core competencies were subject to erosion: what was advanced one day could very well, in today's rapidly changing world, be out-of-date by tomorrow. He thought about the Printing and die-cutting technology, which had served his company very well in the past, but offered little hope for the future. The Graphic design competence would soon be available to almost everybody with a computer. And he knew there were whiz-kids out there who could provide intellectual entertainment in a way that nobody could imagine at the moment.

If Tom Hoffman were honest, he thought, he would have to admit that none of his core competencies offered him any certainty about sustainability. And this caused him considerable concern.

Testing for sustainability

Tom Hoffman's situation is not unique. Many companies – more than would like to admit the fact – are faced with a lack of sustainability. Market circumstances change. Technology is learned by competitors. Supply chain management techniques are copied – and sometimes improved – by eager newcomers. New outlets – such as internet and e-commerce – can threaten existing suppliers. An analysis of core competencies can show us where we can succeed for at least the foreseeable future.

The checklist again contains five questions which you should answer about each of your core competencies to decide whether they can help you retain your competitive advantage into the future. We list them here:

- Is this core competence scarce in your particular branch?
- If competitors wanted to develop this core competence, would that require high investments in time and/or money from them?
- Are underlying parts of the core competence protected by patents, trademarks and other legal measures?
- Is this competence the result of a combination of a number of intangibles, such as skills, knowledge, processes, and corporate culture which cannot be easily copied by the competitors?
- Is this competence unavailable to the competition through acquisition or by using external suppliers or experts in this field or by licensing?

On the surface, this discussion about sustainability may seem very similar to those dealing with competitiveness. Yet there is a very clear distinction which we make: competitiveness deals with the present situation; sustainability deals with the length of time a company can enjoy the competitive advantage. It provides you with a time-scale in which you can work. It tells you how long you can enjoy the advantage before the competitors catch up. This idea that the competitors can catch up was highlighted by the Chairman of Volvo at a product introduction in the mid-1980s. He pointed out to the dealers that Volvo had a competitive edge thanks to its image as a very safe car. But he warned that it would not be long before the rest of the industry provided all the safety features which, at that time, set Volvo apart from its competitors. Today, safety is a given in the automobile industry and the Chairman of Volvo has been proved correct.

Many companies have found themselves in a similar situation, and the successful ones have taken measures to ensure competitiveness in the future. BMW, for example, was initially successful thanks to the quality of its engines

– as its name Bayerische Motoren Werke stresses. Today, however, its success is very much due to its image as a leading marque. The brand identity and image plays a much greater role in the success of BMW than its still high quality engines. But how has the company achieved this image? It has managed to combine very successfully three separate competencies: first, the ability to build tailor-made, high quality models on a single production line; second, the ability to consciously focus on a very specific group of motorists; and third, the ability to achieve a very high technical quality in its cars. This strong combination provides BMW with a high degree of sustainability.[17]

Another example from the automobile branch is that of Honda. It realized that its specific competence was in the field of engines and transmissions, rather than just in automobiles. And so it set up a series of independent sales channels, through which it sells automobiles, motorcycles, boats, and lawn-mowers. By expanding its activities into a range of allied areas, it has been able to achieve sustainable growth for the company. This example demonstrates very clearly how important it is to distinguish a competence from a market; if Honda had considered itself a motorbike manufacturer, rather than a specialist in engines and transmissions, then it would now be a very different – and arguably far less successful – operation.[18]

Honda found success by exploiting existing competencies in new market areas; a similar success story is that of Montell Polyolefins, a world-wide leader in polypropylene resins.

The polypropylene market was traditionally a commodity market – standard products offered for low prices. This was understandable, as the product was a standard thermoplastic used for food packaging, children's toys, and similar applications. Although there are various grades of polypropylene, these were not differentiated in product performance, and therefore everything was treated as a commodity product. Success in this market depended on an economy of scale, which in turn required enormous investments.

In the 1980s Montell decided to break out of this situation. It distinguished a number of gaps in the price/performance curve between polypropylenes and higher priced polymers and engineering plastics. A potential market for high-grade polypropylenes – which would allow customers to replace higher priced, over-engineered products with cheaper alternatives – was defined. Montell had specific competencies in the fields of catalysis and polymer application technology, and the company felt that these competencies could be leveraged in order to produce advanced polypropylene products, and continued development after most of its competitors had stopped. The result was a series of products which contributed to breaking the low-price curve in which polypropylene had been entrapped for so long. Today, Montell has further enhanced its technological leadership in polypropylene and enjoys higher prices for its products, higher profitability, and a world-leadership position.[19]

In the 1980s, Grasso was a highly successful and respected manufacturer of compressor and cooling equipment. Despite this strong reputation – and several major international prizes for entrepreneurial excellence – the company went into a slow decline in the 1990s and seemed destined for Chapter Five. An injection of capital saved the company, but it was obvious that a new strategy would be needed to revert the decline.

A detailed analysis of the company revealed that several of the past diversifications were not in line with the company's core competencies, and that it would be necessary to develop new competencies in certain areas – or develop the existing competencies to a higher level of expertise – if the trend were to be rectified.

With this analysis in mind, Grasso went to work and achieved some spectacular results:

- First, it re-established its position as a world-class manufacturer of compressors. This had been recognized as one of the most important markets for the company, and considerable effort was expended on regaining the lead in it. Grasso drastically increased the production of compressors and built up a full range, thanks to several important acquisitions.

- Second, it recognized the need for a strong sales organization in emerging markets. Developing economies have a large demand for cooling installations, and if Grasso was to be successful in such markets, it would need a highly efficient sales organization to service the existing need and help develop new sales opportunities. Thanks to a drastic overhaul of its sales operations, Grasso was once again able to claim a world-class position.

- And third, it developed a dedicated cooling installation technology, which allowed the company to offer customers world-wide support in engineering, installation, and service. This required the company to improve the systems already in place and harmonize the activities of various business units into a single competence. This has greatly improved the company's robustness – and we shall be returning to this in a moment – in a market which only has room for a limited number of international players.

These three actions have turned Grasso from a potential loser into a potentially long-term winner.

⌐ How robust is Pieces of Fun?

Tom Hoffman pushed aside his sustainability checklist and pulled the final one towards him. As he read through the list of questions, his face brightened a little. He realized that many of the core competencies – in particular the Printing and die-cutting technology and Intellectual entertainment – were firmly rooted in the company. They had a long tradition within the company and had become a part of the company's culture. He was, though, less sure about the robustness of the Graphic design competence: this was relatively new and was an area which was subject to enormous changes, either through technology, taste, or fashion. What's more, his company's "experts" in this field were computer whiz-kids; the competence had not spread throughout the company, but was seen as the property of a few specialists. And, Tom acknowledged, they didn't really fit in. They dressed differently, kept irregular hours, and seemed indifferent to other parts of the company. But they were nevertheless

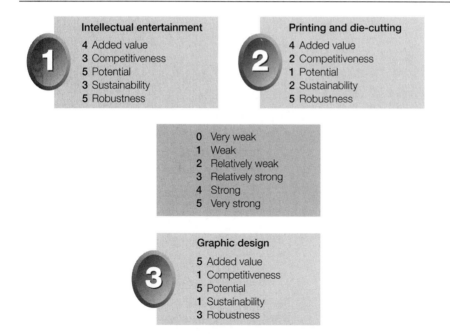

Fig. 4.2 ■ Strengths and weaknesses of Pieces of Fun

important to the company. And, he knew, in great demand. This fact alone made them vulnerable: competitors could quite easily make them an offer they couldn't refuse, and this important competence would simply walk out of the door.

Assessing robustness

In our checklist, we look at things in a reverse manner, and first discover how vulnerable each core competence is.

The questions we must ask to discover how vulnerable each of our core competencies is (or isn't) are the following:

- Is the group of people which possess the skills and knowledge crucial for this competence vulnerable?

- Are the values and norms on which this competence is built under pressure?

- Are the technology and IT systems which form part of this competence vulnerable?

- Are the primary and management processes which this competence uses unreliable?

- Are the endowments this core competence depends on (like the corporate image or the installed client base) vulnerable?

By answering these questions, a score can be obtained which should then be deducted from 5 to give us a robustness score. The intention of this exercise is to help give you a better insight into the robustness of various factors within your company: the human factor (skills, implicit knowledge, and culture), the organizational factor (management processes, and explicit knowledge and skills), and the assets and endowments (image, customer relationships, and networks).

Additional input for determining the robustness score can be found in the personnel policy, and in measurements on staff turnover and employee loyalty. Documentation which shows that efforts have been made to turn implicit knowledge into explicit knowledge, and that measures have been put in place to guard against possible calamities can also help with this exercise.

The importance of determining the robustness of a competence is underlined by a survey carried out in the United Kingdom among a large number of CEOs. They were asked to access how long would be needed to replace a particular intangible asset. Here are the scores:

- Company reputation: 14 years

- Product reputation: 6 years

- Employee know-how: 4 years

- Networks: 4 years

- Supplier know-how: 4 years

- Databases: 3 years

- Distribution know-how: 2 years.[20]

Earlier in this chapter we mentioned the danger of people "joining the enemy": ING Barings bank experienced exactly this when the majority of its dealers accepted jobs with one of the bank's main competitors.[21]

The absence of robustness is – poignantly for some – clearly demonstrated by the decline and virtual disintegration of the once great Imperial Chemicals Industries, ICI. The company started its activities between the two world wars, when the market for chemical products was nicely divided into a number of regions, each dominated by a single player. Du Pont had the North American market; Hoechst, Bayer, and BASF, then operating together as IG-Farben, dominated Europe; and British-based ICI ruled the countries of the British Empire. Each of these three giants concentrated on its own market, and competition between the three was non-existent. It was a highly comfortable position for them all.

But then the world changed. The British Empire fell into decline and ICI began depending for growth on its ability to innovate the production process. Research chemistry was the key to success. And this proved successful: ICI was able to produce products 10–15% cheaper than its competitors. But by the 1970s, the world had changed again. As Middle East and Eastern European producers entered the market, this 10–15% became irrelevant. ICI saw the bulk market for chemicals, which depended on the company's core competence to innovate the production process, reach maturity; but rather than switching its attentions to its pharmaceutical division, it continued on the same course. Investments were channelled away from life sciences to further process innovation in production processes and new plants for a commodity product. Eventually, in 1993, the pharmaceutical and agrochemical businesses were spun off and in 1997, the company diverted into specialty chemicals and announced that it planned to dispose of its basic chemicals business. This it did – but not until 1999, when it was sold to Huntsmen of the US. Today, only the old paints business remains, together with the specialty chemical operation acquired in 1997. For the rest, ICI has become an empty shell, peopled by embittered employees who, according to the retiring head of employees relations, Robin Cook, "cannot wait to get out." A sorry end to a once great company.

This idea of diversifying when a core business comes under attack is seldom successful: American Express discovered this to its dismay when it launched the Optima card – a credit card which, unlike the traditional Amex products, offered consumers the chance of rolling over unpaid balances, proved a financial disaster. Amex did not have sufficient knowledge nor experience in the credit market and miscalculated the adverse effect of defaulters and delinquent debtors. The result: write-offs to the extent of $150 million, and a quarterly loss for the prestigious Travel Related Services division.[22]

People Express – the low-cost, no-frills airline company – became a victim of its own success. As demand for its cheap seats grew, the rudimentary information systems proved inadequate, so that managers could no longer set the right prices to maximize profit. The airline folded after just six years.[23]

⌐ What chance for Pieces of Fun?

Tom Hoffman looked at the results of his five checklists. Was his company in good shape? Certainly there were areas which seemed promising. But there were also areas where he knew the company was vulnerable.

Did he like the results? Perhaps the best description is that he had mixed feelings. But at least he had a better insight into his company than before he started the analysis.

In the coming chapters, we'll see what Tom does with all his newly acquired knowledge.

5

Tom Hoffman leaned back in his chair and stared out of the window. He had the feeling that he was moving in the right direction. He had identified his company's strategically important intangibles by defining three core competencies. He had learned a lot about their relative strengths and weaknesses. But he still had some questions the answers to which would offer him even more insight to his company and the strategy he should adopt.

He turned back to his desk and pulled his notepad towards him. He always found that it helped him get his thoughts in order by writing them down. Taking a freshly sharpened pencil from the supply he always kept on his desk, he began writing.

Across the top of the page he wrote, in capitals, "QUESTIONS THAT NEED AN ANSWER."

He thought for a moment, then wrote his first remark: "How important are the various core competencies for the company's current position?"

His analysis had certainly given him a lot of information about various aspects of the three core competencies he had defined. But he still had little idea which of these offered him the most opportunities for the future. When he had filled in the checklists, he had noticed that all of them had pros and cons. What he wanted to know was which of the core competencies was the most important for his current strategy.

He thought for a moment, then wrote down his next question: "Which core competence should I invest in?"

This was an important question, he knew. The more so because he didn't have an unlimited amount of money at his disposal. Perhaps, he acknowledged with a wry smile, he wouldn't be in this position if he had!

He knew there were a lot of choices he could make. Should he invest more money in machinery, so that he could upgrade further his Printing and die-cutting technology? Should he invest in more sophisticated computers, so that his designers could develop even more challenging games? Should he use his limited resources to invest in hard assets, or should he concentrate on softer assets?

And this brought him to his third question: "How much are my assets really worth?"

He knew that his core competencies were of significant value to his company. Yet they did not appear on his balance sheet. To all intents and purposes, they were worth nothing. But he knew that couldn't be the case. The financial statements made no mention of the core competencies, but did this mean they were worth nothing? Were the financial statements right in ignoring them – because it only dealt with financial matters – or did the exclusion of a value for his core competencies mean that there was a large hole in the information contained in the report?

Tom leaned back and considered this conundrum. Did the competencies have a value? Certainly not in the traditional idea of tangible assets. But that didn't mean they were worthless. He thought deeply for a moment and then his eyes brightened. The value, he suddenly realized, was not in the costs, but in the application. The core competencies had to be used, and that was when they became valuable to the company. In other words, he asked himself, just how much gross profit could be generated in the future thanks to these competencies?

That, he knew, was a key question that he, as manager, needed to know. He wanted to know not so much the intrinsic value of a competence – that would be interesting, but purely as an exercise; no, what he needed to know as a manager was how much profit a competence, and its successful application, could generate.

⊡ The goose that lays the golden egg

Wouldn't it be nice if your company actually owned one of these rare creatures? The question we inevitably ask is: what is the value of one of these remarkable birds?

One way of giving the bird a value would be to say that the value of the goose is determined by its *historical* costs – the costs you incurred in hatching it and raising it. These would include the costs of purchasing a mother goose, the mating, the housing for the goose, and the feed and attention given to your new acquisition.

Another way would be to ask yourself what the *market value* of the goose is. This would depend on whether the buyer was actually convinced that the goose in question would indeed lay golden eggs.

A third way would be to ask yourself what *earnings* you would make from the golden eggs laid during the goose's active lifetime. In other words, the future cash flow and the chances that the goose will continue producing golden eggs.

We think everybody would agree that the third option is the one that really matters.

Strangely enough, though, traditionally companies are only allowed to value their assets using one of the other two methods described here.

But here lies a great danger: intangibles *must* be treated differently to tangibles. And certainly, as we move further into the knowledge economy, those companies which continue accounting intangibles in an old-fashioned way, may very well find to their dismay, that they no longer count in the real world.

When looking at intangibles – and their value – we must concentrate on the revenue streams which they can generate. This is where their true value lies. As Paul Strassman wrote: "The value of intellectual property is in its use, not in its costs."[1]

In his book *The Treatment of Intangibles*,[2] T. H. Donaldson underlines the importance of cash flow for investors. He writes: "To an equity investor the two most important sources of value are the ability to generate cash flow, and sales value. The loss of these in liquidation, important if not overwhelming to a creditor, is of minor importance to a shareholder, since he had almost certainly lost all value by that stage anyway. Most important of all to an equity investor, however, is the ability to keep a company well away from any question of insolvency. Unless sold, it can only do this by generating cash flow to service debt and meet capital and other requirements, including R&D and development interest, to keep the company healthy."

Valuing added value and competitiveness

Tom looked again at the checklists he had filled in. His eye fell on the scores for "Intellectual entertainment." He saw that they were high for both the value added test and the competition test. So, he thought, it must follow that this competence must generate quite a large profit. If it has considerable added value for customers and customers can't get it anywhere else, they will be willing to pay a lot of money which must result in a extensive gross profit.

But did it?

The problem is, Pieces of Fun is not selling its core competencies directly, it is selling products that are manufactured using the core competencies. His company made products in four areas: computer games, board games, puzzle books, and jigsaw puzzles. He clearly saw that the Intellectual entertainment competence was an essential factor for the success of the first two – computer games and board games. But he thought it was much less important for puzzle books, and even less so for jigsaw puzzles. The Printing and die-cutting competence, on the other hand, made an absolutely essential contribution to the success of jigsaw puzzles, but was of no significance whatsoever for computer games.

Looking at the lists in front of him he suddenly had an idea: if he could somehow assess the contribution a competence had to each product group, he could then allocate the gross profits of these product groups to the various competencies and see which competence had the most impact across the board.

Again pulling his pad towards him, he drew a matrix. On one side he listed his company's three core competencies; across the top he listed the four product areas in which his company was active. Using a scoring method, by which he gave three points to the competence which made an essential contribution to the product, down to zero points if it made no contribution at all, he began filling in the matrix. For jigsaw puzzles he thought the Printing and die-cutting technology was essential, so he gave that a score of three. Graphic design, he felt, made a supporting contribution, as did Intellectual entertainment, so he gave both of these one point each. Puzzle books produced a different picture: the Printing and die-cutting technology made no contribution here whatsoever, earning it zero points. Graphic design made a supporting contribution – good for one point – and intellectual entertainment made a substantial contribution – a two. Board games produced yet another picture: a two for Printing and die-cutting, a two for Graphic design, and a three for Intellectual entertainment. And finally, computer games had a zero for Printing and die-cutting, and a three for both Graphic design and Intellectual entertainment.

With the matrix complete, Tom was about to allocate the gross profits to each of the core competencies according to the contribution they made to the individual products. His calculations looked like this:

	Jigsaw puzzles	Puzzle books	Board games	Computer games	Contribution to profits	Percentage
Gross profit	$11.8 m	$6.7 m	$1.3 m	$12.9 m	$32.7 m	100%
Printing and die-cutting	60%	0%	29%	0%	$7.5 m	23%
Graphic design	20%	33%	29%	50%	$11.4 m	35%
Intellectual entertainment	20%	67%	42%	50%	$13.8 m	42%
Total	100%	100%	100%	100%	$32.7 m	100%

Tom looked at the figures he had produced and shook his head in disbelief. He had never realized so much of the success – the profit – of his company depended on its capacity for providing creative and challenging forms of intellectual enter-tainment. The importance of his design team was put into a new perspective! Although he realized that they were not alone in contributing to this competence.

But as he looked at the figures, he recognized that, although Intellectual entertainment was the leader, the other competencies could not be disregarded, as they contributed 35% and 23% to his company's gross profits. Although the three competencies contributed different percentages to his company's success, the differences were fairly narrow. And he knew that other aspects – such as the material and financial assets of the company – also made a contribution to gross profits. For this reason, Tom included a 5% compensation for the average cost of invested capital for these assets in his calculation. In the appendix we give full details of his calculations.

One thing that he noticed was that the competence which scored highest on added value and competitiveness – Intellectual entertainment – was also the competence which contributed most to his company's gross profit.

Calculating potential, sustainability, and robustness

All this gave Tom the answer to his first question: "How important are the various core competencies for the company's current position?" He also wanted to know what the future potential earning power was for each of his core competencies. So he decided to look at the other criteria he had assessed them against: potential, sustainability, and robustness – all things which had to do with the future.

Reaching into a drawer in his desk, he pulled out his company's sales projections for the coming three years. Using these figures, he calculated how much each of the three core competencies would contribute to the growth in gross profits.

The results were astonishing.

Based on his calculations, the potential for Printing and die-cutting was negative: -4%! This meant that, given his company's current portfolio, the Printing and die-cutting competence had a negative effect on growth.

All this raised a question in his mind: should he move the business more determinedly into the field of graphic design? Or should he invest in finding new applications for the Printing and die-cutting technology which had been the source of the company's success for so many years. He decided to put his problem aside for the moment, hoping that looking at the other areas may give him more information. He wrote down "Sustainability" on his notepad. Just how sustainable was the success of his company? He thought about this and realized that there was considerable cause for concern in this area.

Part of his concern was the complete unpredictability of the toy market. At the moment, his customers seemed very happy with the products he was offering, his company was stable, and profits were reasonable. But what would happen if a competitor came up with something totally new, totally original? He had no way of knowing what the market would demand in ten or even five years from now. This was not the time for complacency.

He looked at his list of core competencies and realized that he should be modest. They where generating a good gross profit now, but this could change in only a few years. In fact he would need to sort of "depreciate" the intangibles in the same way he depreciated tangible assets in his company. The question was: how? Looking down the Sustainability checklist he decided that he could only count on the earning capacity of his core competencies in the length of time a competitor would need to acquire that competence, thus robbing him of his competitive edge. He looked at the three and thought for a moment. Graphic design was, he felt, the most vulnerable – with the speed of technological progress, he thought a competitor could gain this competence in just a single year. The Printing and die-cutting technology was more demanding. In his company, it was the result of many years' work and dedication. But he thought that a determined competitor could match this competence in two years. The Intellectual entertainment competence was, perhaps, the most difficult for a competitor to develop, but he knew that a single-minded competitor could build up the same competence in just three years.

The short time-span he had allocated to each of his core competencies showed, yet again, that he had no time for complacency.

He turned now to finding a way of assessing the robustness of his competencies. Were they really anchored into his organization? Could he be sure his company would have the competencies for the foreseeable future? Were any of his competencies at risk?

He looked at them again. He decided that Printing and die-cutting was firmly anchored in the organization. It was the competence which had made the company successful and he saw no way of it ever being at risk. He thought about Intellectual entertainment, and felt that much the same could be said about that. He believed, on analysis, that there was no risk to his company of losing either of these competencies, since many people contributed to them and all were loyal to Pieces of Fun.

Graphic design was a different matter. It was the newest of the three competencies and mastered by only a handful of employees. What's more, there was a high demand in the market for graphic design specialists and he acknowledged that his specialists might be tempted away with the offer of large salary increases. On consideration, he thought that he should take into account a risk of 40% of losing this competence.

⊏⅂ The value of intangibles

Tom looked at the notes he had made on his pad and leaned back in his chair. He felt he was very close to discovering something important. He had, he realized, an enormous amount of information about his core competencies – about their strengths and weaknesses, about the contribution they made to gross profits, about the growth they could give, and the length of time that earning capacity could be continued. And he also knew the risk of losing each of his competencies.

But did all this bring him any closer to establishing the value of each competence? He thought it must do – but he had to find a way of calculating that value.

He tried various formulae until he hit on one so simple that he at first doubted whether it could be true. But on considering its implications he realized that this was the correct way. He smiled: all he had to do to find the value of each individual core competence was to multiply together the various factors he had listed.

In other words, the value of a core competence = added value × competitiveness × potential × sustainability × robustness.

He looked at the formula and smiled. For he realized the implications. It meant that the value a core competence adds to a company equals the added value for the customer under the current competitive situation, the growth that can be expected thanks to this competence over the coming years, and the number of years the competence can be exploited. The result was then corrected by the risk of losing a competence prematurely. As he was interested in the present value of each competence, he knew he should include a discount factor, which he decided should be equal to the average cost of invested capital: 5%.

With this formula in mind, Tom now set about calculating the present value for each of his company's core competencies. He started with the value of Printing and die-cutting technology.

He looked at the figures on the various sheets of paper. In 1999, this competence had contributed $7.5 million to his company's gross profits. The factor for potential was –4%, the sustainability two years, and the robustness 100%.

He listed his calculations in a table he drew on a new sheet of paper.

Year	Contribution to gross profits	Discount factor of 5%	Present value
2000	7.2	95.2%	6.9
2001	6.9	90.7%	6.2
2002	–		–
Total			**13.1**
Correction for robustness			–
Total present value			**13.1**

Table 5.2 ■ Present value of Printing and die-cutting (in US$ millions)

He now turned to intellectual entertainment. In 1999, this competence had contributed $13.8 million to his company's gross profits. The factor for potential was 10% and the sustainability was three years. The robustness was, again, 100%.

He now entered his calculations into a fresh chart.

Year	Contribution to gross profits	Discount factor of 5%	Present value
2000	15.2	95.2%	14.5
2001	16.7	90.7%	15.1
2002	18.4	86.4%	15.9
Total			**45.5**
Correction for robustness			–
Total present value			**45.5**

Table 5.3 ■ Present value of Intellectual entertainment (in US$ millions)

Finally he drew a new table and began calculating the value of Graphic design. This competence had made a contribution of $11.4 million to gross profits in 1999. Its potential factor was 13%, but it had a sustainability of just one year. What's more, it had a high risk factor – its robustness was only 60%.

Year	Contribution to gross profits	Discount factor of 5%	Present value
2000	12.9	95.2%	12.3
2001	–		–
2002	–		–
Total			12.3
Correction for robustness			4.9
Total present value			7.4

Table 5.4   Present value of Graphic design (in US$ millions)

He now listed the totals for the three competencies under each other, so that he could calculate their total value to the company.

Competence	Value to Pieces of Fun
Printing and die-cutting	US$ 13.1 m
Intellectual entertainment	US$ 45.5 m
Graphic design	US$ 7.4 m
Total value of core competencies	US$ 66.0 m

Sixty-six million dollars! He could hardly believe his eyes. That was nearly three times as much as his tangible assets.

He sat back, his mind swaying back and forth between elation and concern. He was pleased that his competencies were worth so much to his company. But he was concerned that so much of the value of his company was in things he couldn't touch and which partly walked out of the office every single evening. More than 75% of the value of his company was walking around unprotected, and there was no way he could lock it up for safe keeping!

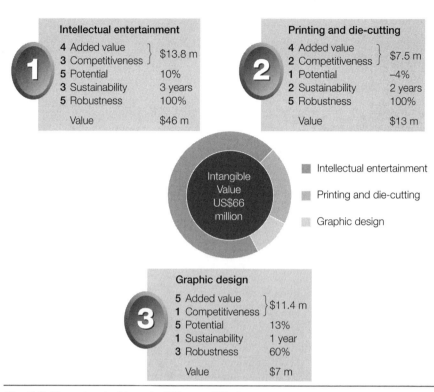

Fig. 5.6 The value dashboard of Pieces of Fun

Knowing the value of core competencies is the first step towards managing them

The conundrum facing Tom is one which faces every single manager today. You want to manage your intangibles – but how can you possibly manage something which you cannot see, hear, smell, or touch? And the worry is only aggravated when you see the hard figures for these "soft" assets in front of you.

Yet these hard figures can be of incalculable value in your decision-making process about investments.

Until now, much of the investment ploughed into matters such as training, knowledge management, R&D, improvement of internal and external communications, and company co-operation have generally been based on your gut feeling. You knew you had to make investments in these areas, but had few facts to justify your decisions.

By analyzing your core competencies and discovering the contribution each makes to the profits of your company, you can get a much clearer – much more tangible – idea about those intangibles which have the greatest value for your company. You can then use your investments for strategic reasons – whether to improve competitiveness, sustainability, or so on.

Betsey Nelson, the 38-year-old CFO of software giant Macromedia, knows all about the value of intangibles. "Everything we do is intangible; the top line, the bottom line, *everything* is intangible."[3] She admits that her number one concern is "people assets." Without the people in the company – the designers and developers who have created such industry-standard packages as Director, Flash, Fireworks, and Dreamweaver – Macromedia would have nothing more than an office building in Silicon Valley.

A major project at the moment underway at Macromedia is code-named: "The New Way." This is an internal investment program aimed at shifting much of the company's business onto the web. Despite its enormous presence on the web, Macromedia still does 75% of its business through traditional channels such as dealers and distributors. The New Way aims at creating a new "neighborhood" in cyberspace which will concentrate on all aspects of the business process – from creating customer awareness, through sales, to support and service.

A detailed plan for The New Way was developed, which seemed to satisfy all the requirements for transferring customer contacts to the web.

But there was one question left answered: what was The New Way worth? A decision was taken to measure the value of the project in three areas: marketing return on investment; the cost of sales; and share of customer loyalty.

This last one proved to be the hardest of the three areas. Customer loyalty is one of those typical intangibles which are hard to translate into hard figures. Yet Nelson finally produced figures which reflected cost cuts, increased conversions, increased loyalty, and revenues from new products. Although, as Nelson pointed out, the project remained a venture investment – combining high risk with high reward – the analysis showed her exactly how important it was for Macromedia to learn just how important customer relationships were for them.[4]

Supporting your feelings

A second important aspect of knowing the value of your intangibles is that it can help stimulate a more open discussion about them. Many companies –

and many managers – still feel safer when they are dealing with hard figures. Financial results still have a priority in many management decisions. This often leads to a climate in which it is almost impossible to discuss investments in people. Simply because a financial price-tag cannot be attached to them. "That's just a feeling – and we cannot run a company on feelings."

Now there *is* a way of calculating the value of people and the contribution they make to the profits. By confronting an otherwise financially-oriented management with financial figures about intangibles, it makes the discussion much easier and more understandable for them. Once, like Tom, they see just how large the contribution of intangibles is to the company's performance, they are more likely to adapt their investment strategy accordingly.

> "What can be measured is not always important, and what is important cannot always be measured."

All this cannot happen overnight. It requires a change in management attitude. Traditionally they have relied on things which can be measured, and have written off as unimportant anything which cannot be measured. But we should be reminded of the words of Albert Einstein: "What can be measured is not always important, and what is important cannot always be measured."[5]

Resisting short-term pressures

And third, the process we have described can show the value of investments which provide return in a medium term. This is important in a culture which is constantly concentrating on short-term results.

We have to admit, though, that much of this pressure comes from sources over which companies have little control. There is an unprecedented volatility in the capital markets, which is forcing companies to concentrate on short-term returns. Until just a few years ago, it was rare for a company to publish its quarterly results; today it is a matter of course. The impact of these quarterly figures are such that management could be excused from its short-term thinking. But nevertheless, it is important for the continuity of a company to consider its middle- and long-term investments and strategies. These are largely in the field of investments in intangibles – in training, IT, and so on – but they cannot, because of the short-term pressures, be ignored. Reporting the value of intangibles can be an important weapon in showing the market that investments in them are of importance to the value of the company. If a company can show that its intangibles make a significant contribution to its profits, then it has a better defense against the pressure for short-term thinking.

Today, we hear a lot about "shareholder value" – and we must admit that this is the very embodiment of short-term thinking. For by concentrating on shareholder value, managers prefer to ignore anything – including vital investments – which could have an adverse effect on financial statements.

One area where short-term thinking has often be prevalent is in the management of pension funds. In a determination to achieve the best possible return on investment, many fund managers are willing to buy and sell stocks with an indifference to the effect such dealings could have on the company involved.

The California Public Employees' Retirement System (CalPERS) has adopted a different approach. It prefers to manage about 75% of its investments passively; it holds the best stocks and the worst stock rather than selling stocks out of hand. CalPERS, however, realized that it was important to achieve greater turn across the board, and has adopted a highly untraditional approach which is aimed at helping under-performing companies in its portfolio – and it deals with some 1,700 stocks worth around $100 billion – perform better.

Since the mid-1980s, a "focus list" of the "worst" underachievers has been drawn up – generally containing the names of ten companies – and an analysis made of the reasons behind the company's inability to perform well. It then approaches the company and asks it to take steps to perform better in the specified areas.

Some ten years ago, CalPERS caused something of a sensation by suggesting that boards of management should modernize their governance in order to improve performance. The argument was that if the board was simply an old boys' club, with friends of the CEO who were prepared to rubber-stamp any decision he might make, then a feeling throughout the company could be created which said "good enough" is good enough.

The suggestion was not greeted with enthusiasm. Many CEOs stated that they simply did not believe that something as intangible as governance could have any influence whatsoever on a company's earning abilities.

CalPERS did not back down. They were convinced that intangibles such as directorial independence and board practices which concentrated on accountability to the shareholders, were very good indicators of long-term value. With this in mind, CalPERS asked those companies on its focus list to appoint a majority of independent directors, to forbid poison-pill takeover-protection plans, to pay directors only with stock and cash, and to evaluate their own and their CEO's performance against written criteria.

This concentration on an intangible such as governance has proved highly successful – companies that rethink their governance practices do increase in value. And this is proved conclusively by the figures. The stock price of 62 companies targeted by CalPERS on its focus list trailed the Standards & Poors 500 Index by 89% in the five years before the CalPERS initiative. Within a few years of that initiative, these same companies outperformed the S&P's average returns by 23%.

CalPERS believe that an enlightened board, with good governance practices in place, is one of the strongest indicators of that company's performance.[6]

Reporting on value

Although we have discussed the need for management to use figures for internal improvements, there can be occasions when a company is forced into placing a value on its intangibles in order to give a proper picture of its true worth. This can be important, for example, when a take-over bid is made. Then the company making the bid needs to have a very detailed picture of a company's worth and potential value.

Nortel Networks, once specialized in producing hardware to run telephone networks, has more recently been establishing itself as a leading force on the web, installing internet protocol networks that can carry both voice and data. Its vision: to create a web-tone as reliable as the dial tone which was once the symbol of the company's success.

It was obvious that Nortel did not have all the knowledge or technology required for its new role, and it began an aggressive acquisition policy to acquire the intangibles it would need to become the leader in its chosen field. And the experiences in these acquisitions has taught the company the importance of placing a true value on an acquisition candidate, not least in the field of its intangibles.

An example of this is shown in the acquisition of Aptis Communications, a start-up company in Massachusetts which had developed an access switch capable of handling three times as many dial-ins as the highest volume modem then available. For Nortel, with its web-tone vision, Aptis was a very attractive acquisition target indeed. It could open up a whole new market to it – if it were first to market. For Nortel had learnt that speed in this business – or rather being faster to market than competitors – was a way to generate high profits. According to Klaus Buechner, the company's senior vice president of corporate strategy and alliances, being first brings huge benefits – even if "first" isn't the absolute best.

Aptis offered Nortel the chance to be first with a product which would give the company a six-months lead over competition. The question was: what value should be placed on Aptis? This was difficult, because Aptis had no product whatsoever and the development of its access switch was less than 90% complete.

A rule of thumb for valuing such companies had once been suggested by John Chambers, CEO of Cisco Systems. This said that each engineer in the company was worth $2 million. There were 40 engineers at Aptis, so, according to Chambers' formula, the company was worth $80 million. Was this a realistic figure for the people and the knowledge that was exclusively in their heads?

It was obviously in the interests of both Aptis and Nortel to arrive at some figure which represented not only the knowledge in the minds of the engineers, but also the business benefits which would result in beating the competition to market. Nortel calculated the revenues that were likely to come from the sale of the Aptis product through Nortel's marketing and sales channels. Although a discounted cash-flow analysis was made, Nortel acknowledged that it had its shortcomings in such cases. For success depended on other things, including leveraging channels, getting product to market, and customer relationships.

Aptis looked at its own value in a slightly different way. First, it looked at comparable initial public offerings on Wall Street. And second, it calculated the possible future earnings of Aptis, discounted them, and multiplied them by the price-earnings ratio of comparable high-growth public companies.

Although seemingly dissimilar, both approaches acknowledged one key matter: speed. Being first to market would give them a major advantage in selling product to telecom companies and a big head start in cash flow.

Ultimately, Nortel acquired Aptis for the record price for a start-up company with no product of $290 million. An enormous gamble, but one which is clearly paying off. Not only did Aptis deliver on time, but it is actually lengthening its lead over competition to between nine and twelve months.[7]

⊡ Your intangibles are worth as much as your next great idea

Today there is no shortage of knowledge. It can be accumulated from almost everywhere. What's more, knowledge doesn't get "used up"; it doesn't wear out. But knowledge as such is of little value. It's what we do with it that counts. The same piece of knowledge can mean nothing to one company, yet can mean millions of dollars to another.

All this raises the question of whether it is possible to determine a single value for the future potential of knowledge or other intangibles. And to determine it objectively.

Knowledge as such can be seen as an asset. But it only has value when it is applied. The future cash flow in an economy such as today's – where success is determined by speed, innovation, and added value – depends on how successfully a company is able to apply the knowledge it has.

> The future cash flow in an economy such as today's ... depends on how successfully a company is able to apply the knowledge it has.

It thus follows that the value of knowledge – indeed the value of all intangibles – depends on a company's view of the market and its own strength in being able to play a decisive role in that market. If a company is able to understand market opportunities and find applications which offer added value for its customers, then the value of intangibles will be higher than similar intangibles in a company which is *not* able to leverage market opportunities and offer added value for customers.

All companies experience R&D failures. 3M was one such company. It developed an adhesive which didn't stick. A failure. Back to the drawing board would have been the most common reaction. In fact, the value of the know-how that resulted from R&D was worth a couple of million in terms of historic costs, and zero in terms of economic potential. Yet 3M had a creative idea and applied the adhesive to pads of yellow paper, which allowed people to make notes which they could stick to something and remove later. The success of 3M's failure has generated many millions of dollars in profits on Post-it memos for the company. So the same know-how suddenly was worth millions.

Other companies are faced with enforced obsolescence when a new technology overtakes an existing one. The Dutch Telecom were faced with such an obsolescence when the digital mobile network superseded their existing analog mobile network. Forget the whole thing? Write it off? That was one way of looking at it. But the Dutch Telecom chose a novel perspective: it launched a low-price product aimed at the youth market, which made use of an otherwise obsolete asset. The result? It generated cash flow from its assets and created, at the same time, a strong new brand in the youth market. So strong, in fact, that the same brand is now being applied to digital telephones for the youth market.

These two examples show how the value of knowledge and other intangibles will vary according to the perspective of the company and the way knowledge is applied. Measuring the value of intangibles is like taking a snapshot. What we see on the picture is the value they have for a company in its perspective in a specific moment in time.

☐ The strength of a core competence is a measure of its value

In the previous chapters we helped you define those core competencies in your company which contain those intangibles which are of the greatest strategic importance. We have then shown you how to apply tests to these core competencies which show their relative strengths and weaknesses.

If we look at those tests, then we see quite clearly that there is a direct relationship between the outcome of the tests and the value of your core competencies. The higher the score in the tests, the higher the value of the competence. The value of a core competence – and therefore the value of a company's intangibles – is calculated using the relationship between the strength of a core competence and the value it adds to the company. After all, it is obvious that the higher the customer benefits created by a core competence, the more valuable that competence is. Similarly, the longer a competence is sustainable, the greater its value.

Each of the five tests give some indication of the value of the core competence. But its total value, as Tom Hoffman discovered, is found by multiplying the five indicators together. This gives us the following formula:

Value of core competence (VCC) =
added value × competitiveness × potential × sustainability × robustness

This formula means that the value a core competence adds to a company equals the added value of the core competence for the customer, given the current competitive relationships, the growth that can be expected in the coming years (potential), and the number of years for which it can be exploited (sustainability). This is then corrected by a factor showing whether there is a risk that the company will lose the core competence prematurely (robustness).

Obviously, to make the above calculation, the indicators must be expressed in factors to which a figure can be assigned.

Making each factor visible

On the surface, much of this may seem very theoretical. But that is not the case. It is highly practical. Each of the factors we have determined can be put to work for your company, to ensure that you have better insight into your operations.

Let us look at each of the factors in turn, and see how they can be made visible to you.

Added value and competitiveness

These two factors – added value and competitiveness – may, on the surface, seem to be indicators of total performance rather than of individual core competencies. Yet the opposite is true. Let us explain our reasoning.

If you know that a core competence has "added value" for the customer, then you will also know that it helps your company to sell products and make healthy margins. What's more, your company can also increase its margins by being better than competition. Nortel found this out – it was not only better than the competition, but considerably faster and ahead of it. Customers, therefore, are prepared to pay more for a product which has added value and is better than a product offered by the competition. And your company will be able to generate higher gross profits. If, on the other hand, you discover that a core competence has low added value and is less well-developed than that of the competition, then you can be pretty certain that your competitor will be making the profits rather than you!

> The value of a core competence ... is calculated using the relationship between the strength of a core competence and the value it adds to the company.

We can therefore now say that gross profit is a measure of the added value of a core competence, within the competitive field.

But your core competencies are not the things you sell (unless your company is the target for an acquisition). For daily operations, the core competencies allow you to develop attractive products and services which are – hopefully – successful in the market-place. And that is why we have to see what contribution each core competence makes to your products and services. The first step is to determine the gross profits made from products to which the core competencies contribute. The gross profits can then be divided over the various core competencies – and you can then see the contribution made by added value and competitive advantage.

One question you may be asking is why we chose gross profits for this calculation rather than net margin. We believe gross profits give a clearer picture of the turnover generated by a particular profit without that figure being distorted by overhead costs. We determine the gross profit by deducting the direct costs from the income generated by the product.

It will be obvious that a product is not solely the result of intangibles. There are tangible and financial assets which also make a contribution to the value of a product. Things like production facilities and net working capital. But our intention in our method is to determine the value of *intangibles*. For this reason, the gross profit must be corrected for the return on the net invested capital needed to realize a product or service.

In some cases, you may find that your calculations show that the contribution a core competence makes to a product is a negative value. There can be two explanations for this – and it is important that you decide which is the one applicable in each particular case. On the one hand, the core competence may be reaching the end of its life-cycle, in which case a negative value is perfectly normal. On the other, it may be just at the start of its life-cycle, in which case the investments may far exceed the returns. If this second case is applicable for you, then you must make a prognosis of the realistic gross profit which can be expected in the future.

Potential

The potential of a core competence is made visible through the potential factor. This factor is expressed as an expected growth percentage of gross profit per year. Once again, this factor may prove negative – which is the case when the gross profit is expected to decline, We analyze the past growth and expected growth in the near future to determine a percentage. We also take into account market developments when calculating this percentage.

Sustainability

The sustainability factor is a translation of the "sustainability" indicator, and shows how long your company can sustain its uniqueness over your competition in a particular core competence. The factor is expressed in years.

The sustainability factor is actually a measure of the rate at which your company should "depreciate" the core competence. We all know about depreciation for tangible assets, which is based on the economic working life of the asset concerned. And although intangibles are not "rival assets" – which is generally the case for physical, tangible assets – a form of "depreciation" must still be taken into account because the life of an intangible is equal to the time it would take a competitor to gain the same level of expertise in this intangible, or even surpass it. Depreciation must be a function of your competitive advantage.

Today's knowledge economy is fast and ruthless. A competitive advantage can disappear virtually overnight. If your core competencies are no longer unique, then you lose your right to existence. You merge into the crowd, where profits are minimal at the best. And it is exactly this which we have to take into account when calculating the value of our intangibles: you might suddenly find that the value is zero because you took your eye off competition.

The main implication of the sustainability factor is that the value of a core competence is directly related to the number of years in which that competence is unique within your given market or industry.

If we compare this with the traditional Discounted Cash Flow (DCF) method that is often used to value companies or products, we see a striking difference. DCF stems from the industrial age. With DCF the time period for which the cash flow is forecasted is often very long to infinite. This means when using DCF we assume the cash flow will be generated indefinitely, without taking into account the competitive situation of the company.

This time period is often divided into two periods – the explicit forecast period and the period after the explicit forecast period. This results in a total value – of, for example, a company – being equal to the present value of cash flow *during* a period with an explicit forecast, plus the present value of cash flow *after* a period with an explicit forecast. This last value is called the continuing value, and it often accounts for a large percentage of the total value of a company.[8]

The assumption for the continuing value is that the cash flow will be generated for ever, an assumption that is very unlikely in today's turbulent economy. Instead, in the New Economy, one should be on the safe side with a close eye on the competition. Therefore we should only look at the cash flow that is being generated during those years that a company is unique with its competencies.

Robustness

The robustness factor – which is derived from the robustness indicator – is expressed as a risk percentage. This shows how securely, how firmly, an intangible is embedded in your company. Is it something which permeates all layers of the organization, something which, perhaps, has been around for a long time and has made considerable contributions to the success of your company, or is it restricted to just a few people within the organization? Obviously the risk factor in the first case is far lower than in the second, where there is the possibility that the people involved in the competence can move elsewhere.

What is the present value of a core competence?

Based on the above, we can say that the present value of a core competence is calculated by multiplying all the factors over time, taking into account the cost of invested capital. This gives us the following formula:

$$Vcc = \left[\sum_{t=1}^{S} \frac{GP*(1 + P)^t}{(1 + i)^t} \right] * R$$

$Vcc =$ Value of Core Competence
$S =$ Sustainability (in years)
$GP =$ Gross Profit
$P =$ Potential for the future (in %)
$R =$ Robustness (in %)
$i =$ Cost of capital

In other words, this means that over the life-cycle of a core competence (from $t = 1$ to S) the share of the gross profits (GP) of the core competence in each year is added together, taking into account an increase each year of $P\%$ and a cost of invested capital ($i\%$). This figure is then multiplied by the robustness of the core competence (R).

Now that you have calculated the value of the intangibles in your company, it is important to find a way of putting your new knowledge to your strategic benefit. Let us see how Tom Hoffman goes about doing just that in the next chapter.

6

om Hoffman looked at the many sheets of paper he had filled during his analyses and decided that the time was right to start getting some order into his musings. What he wanted to know was how he could put all the knowledge he had acquired in his thought process into some sort of action plan. It was all very well, he realized, to know the value of the core competencies in his company – but to stop there would make the whole thing a rather pointless operation. What he wanted to know – and what he had wanted to know from the very start – was how he could use all the knowledge he had acquired about his core competencies and the contribution they made to his company's operation, profit, and future to gain competitive advantage. In other words – how could he leverage the potential he now knew was in the company?

He thought for a moment, then decided to use not the competencies but rather the five areas he had discussed – added value, competitive advantage, potential, sustainability, and robustness – to determine the current state of affairs at Pieces of Fun.

Taking a fresh sheet of paper, he wrote *Added Value* at the top. Did his company really provide more added value than its customers expected?

He knew that present customers appreciated the creativity of the games. This was something which had cropped up time and again during his analysis and he knew that in this area the products his company marketed really did add value for the customer. But he knew the market was changing. There was a constant shift away from traditional games and puzzles towards electronic games. His company still had a good reputation for quality and creativity in puzzles, but he knew there was increasing competition from Asia in this area – and he knew that margins in that field would inevitably come under pressure and shrink.

So did all this mean that his company's traditional competencies had run their course and were now superfluous? He didn't think so. But he knew he would have to look long and hard to find new ways of putting these competencies to competitive use.

He now wrote *Competitiveness* on his sheet of paper. He felt the key question he had to ask himself here was how Pieces of Fun could continue to distinguish itself from the competition in the future. Because he knew that if it did not distinguish itself, then it would have lost any competitive advantage it might enjoy now.

He had to acknowledge that Pieces of Fun was, at the moment, a niche player. There was nothing wrong with that – many successful companies were niche players – but he had to acknowledge that the niche was becoming ever smaller. Much of the success of his company was based on its ability to offer quality – largely thanks to its traditional expertise in printing and die-cutting – and on the intellectual content of the games themselves. He knew that intellectual entertainment certainly had a place in the new world of electronic games and so did quality. He felt that these two aspects could be extended into the new market, but he knew he would have to find new ways in which to be unique, particularly as he would no longer be able to base the appeal of his company's products on the "traditional" craftsmanship which had gained them such a following in the past.

He now wrote *Potential* on his sheet of paper. He thought about this for a moment – then decided that the key question he should ask himself was whether his company could create new opportunities with its existing core competencies.

The market was moving away from those areas in which his traditional competence – printing and die-cutting – could provide uniqueness. The importance of this competence, he knew, would decline in the coming years. The question he asked himself was whether he could find new uses for this competence, and if not, whether he could find new applications based on his other two competencies, graphic design and intellectual entertainment. He wondered whether he could make better use of these latter two by forming an alliance with an internet provider to allow his company to develop a sales channel for its games through the web.

He paused for a moment, then wrote *Sustainability*. Was his company in a position to stay ahead of the competition?

His brow furrowed. He knew that his company had done nothing to protect its competencies. There were no patents to protect its printing and die-cutting competence. Perhaps he should look into that and patent those areas which gave his company its present lead.

The world of electronic games was running away with itself. The speed of innovation was incredible – something Pieces of Fun had never come up against in the past. There progress was incremental – now it was revolutionary. He honestly doubted whether his company had the knowledge or the creativity to keep up with the rest of the field – let alone take a lead. If he was really serious about participating in this market as a serious player, he would have to find reinforcements for the competence required elsewhere. An alliance with a software development group could be one answer.

Finally he wrote down *Robustness*. Were his competencies sufficiently anchored in his organization? He had already seen from his previous analysis that his graphic design competence was vulnerable. It was provided by too few people, and that left his company highly exposed. It seemed advisable to strengthen his team in this area. But this, alone, would not ensure robustness. He knew he would also have to think about ways of getting the people committed to the company and ensuring that they would stay with him for a long time.

He sat back, a feeling of despondency falling over him. It was bad. To try to say it was anything else would be stupid. The present financial situation may be good – but there seemed limited perspectives for the future. Unless he took action.

Traditional teaching would tell him to downsize and restructure. This would certainly have a short-term positive effect on his company's profitability – but it seemed to fly in the face of everything Pieces of Fun had always stood for. Its employees had been loyal to the company – and Tom felt that it would be an act of managerial weakness to save the company by dismissing some of its most loyal employees.

No, he thought firmly, he did not plan to take the negative approach. That was the job of an interim manager – not of a manager determined to steer his company into a new future prosperity. He wanted to take a positive approach. This meant he would have to improve the value his products added, his competitiveness, and his potential. He would have to find new products and new areas in which he could exploit his competencies.

His sessions of analysis had convinced him of one very important fact: his intangibles were the life-blood of the company, making an important contribution to its profitability. These intangibles, embedded in core competencies should be nurtured and allowed to flower, even if they had to find new gardens in which to flourish.

Yet he had to remain practical. Sentimentality, he knew, had cost many companies their existence. He was acutely aware that the printing and die-cutting competence was making less contribution to his company than at any time in the past. Many companies in this situation would decide to discontinue its manufacturing activities, preferring to out-source them to a third party. After all, many writers and gurus were maintaining that production belonged to the old "industrial economy," and had little or no place in the new knowledge economy. And although Tom could see the logic of all this, he knew that this old competence was the one which gave his company its identity. To get rid of all production would be like cutting the heart out of Pieces of Fun.

Yet one fact remained valid, no matter what he thought: his analysis had shown that the printing and die-cutting competence had little value in it. And within a few years it would actually have a negative value to his company. Could he afford to ignore the fact that the competence had no value?

Tom felt he was in a true management dilemma: if he got rid of the competence, he would cut the heart out of the company; if he kept the competence he would soon face the negative influence it would have on his income.

As he sat pondering this quandary he suddenly remembered something he had read. It spoke of the "tyranny of OR." That managers had always been raised to believe that a question was always an "either/or" debate, but that frequently it was a question of "and/and".

In this light he saw that there was another way of addressing the problem: to reverse the negative profitability of this competence. If he could improve the added value, competitiveness, and potential for this competence, then he could possibly turn it into something which contributed to his company's profits. Today it might not have much value – but he could, he knew, find ways of giving it value in the future. He could find new ways of making money with this competence.

But how could he do that, given the present circumstances in the world of games and toys? Yet even as he asked the question, he knew that was the wrong way of approaching things. What he had to do was be creative. Look at things from a new angle – from every angle.

He had to think out of the box.

With a smile on his face he picked up the telephone and began making some calls.

◻ Intangibles need to be managed strategically

As Tom discovered through his analysis, analyzing the strengths and weaknesses of your core competencies can provide you with important information which you can use to see how these competencies can positively affect your strategy. In fact, it is essential, when considering your competencies, to realize that it is essential to manage them strategically.

The questions Tom asked himself when reviewing his findings resulted in a management agenda, which helped Tom – and would help you – focus on the strategic issues facing his – your – company.

Let us look again at those questions.

Added value

When looking at this, we have to ask ourselves whether our company continually adds perceivable added value for our customers. Do the things we do, the products we market, the services we offer, go further to meet the expectations of our customers than those of our competitors? Indeed, it is important to ensure that the expectations of our customers are exceeded – for this in itself is a way of adding value for them.

Competitiveness

No company – or only those who are exceptionally fortunate (and this situation rarely lasts very long!) – operates in a vacuum. We all have competitors. And we all know that, in order to be successful, we need to distinguish ourselves from our competitors. The question we need to ask ourselves is whether we can do that – and continue to do that – in both the present circumstances, and in future circumstances, when we may be faced with competitors who newly arrive on the scene with good ideas.

Potential

One of the biggest traps a company can fall into is to continue doing something "because we have always done it that way." It is vital, in a time when there is often never enough time, that we constantly "reinvent" ourselves. Look for new applications for our core competencies. We must ask ourselves whether our core competencies can provide us with new opportunities in the future.

Sustainability

We operate in a world of constant change. Here today – gone tomorrow. Life-cycles decrease. New products appear with alarming regularity. Our competitors do not stand still. We must ask ourselves whether our competencies will help us remain better than the competition. Do we have a healthy lead so that it will take them a long time to catch up? Or are we only marginally better – marginally ahead? How big is the chance that our competitors will catch up – and even overtake us?

Robustness

How anchored is a competence in your company? Is a competence which is of vital importance to your company likely to "get up and leave"? What you have to ask yourself is what measures you have to take to ensure that the competencies you have today are still available tomorrow. Frequently – and increasingly in our present knowledge economy – this will mean paying more attention than ever before to the well-being of your staff.

⊔ Incremental and radical innovation

By now, everybody knows the theory of the growth curve. It was for many years – and still is – something we can use to plot the position our company is in at any stage of its history. Each product and service has its own cycle – often known as the S-curve. This implies that there is initially a period of slow growth, when a product or service is first introduced, then a period of healthy growth, as the product starts enjoying success and the initial investments in R&D and the like have been recouped, and finally a period of maturity, in which the growth levels out before finally declining at the end of the product's life-cycle.

> What you have to ask yourself is what measures you have to take to ensure that the competencies you have today are still available tomorrow.

By now most managers will know that it is essential to introduce new products before the existing product has reached maturity, so that the new product can get through the initial low-growth period while the existing product is still generating a healthy profit. When the initial product goes into decline, the theory says, the new product will have entered its period of healthy growth, thus ensuring on-going income for the company concerned.

The question facing managers, however, is not whether to innovate – that is vital in today's volatile market – but how to do it. And there are two approaches which are open to a manager: radical innovation and incremental innovation.

But there are also risks in this result. A radical innovation takes a company into totally uncharted territory. And this means that initially it will require considerable investments before any returns can be expected. These investments are not only in the development of new technology, but also in the areas of marketing, customer relations, distribution, and so on. A radical innovation may offer the pot of gold at the end of the rainbow – but it can often take a long time to reach that pot.

An incremental innovation can profit from all the previous innovation work done by a company, and therefore it can start its cycle at a much higher level of income than a radical innovation. After all, it makes use of research, development, and marketing and distribution efforts already undertaken for its predecessor.

As we saw with Tom Hoffman, many of us are still enduring the tyranny of "either/or." We have been brought up to believe that there is only ever one possible solution to a problem – it is "either" radical innovation "or" incremental innovation.

In today's world, that is certainly no longer the case. Today, we are frequently faced with "and/and" solutions – and this is particularly true here. A successful strategy will include both incremental change and radical innovation.

⌐ Three steps for success

When it comes to managing intangibles there are three steps which can lead to success:

■ You must learn to leverage the potential in your core competencies and create a strategy in which incremental change and radical innovation are in proper balance. If you handle this successfully, then you will create greater added value, become more competitive, and create greater potential for your company in the future.

■ You must secure your competencies from the competition. If you're ahead, then you must stay ahead. You may decide to patent key areas of your technology to ensure a competitive edge. Whatever you do, you must never stop nurturing your core competencies. Give them the constant attention they deserve and you will create higher sustainability for them.

■ Anchor your competencies in your organization. Here knowledge management is key. This often requires creating an environment in which exchange of knowledge is encouraged. The "ivory tower" mentality of yesterday is even less appropriate or acceptable today. More attention than ever before must be paid to employees – training, education, recognition all become key aspects of today's company strategy. Certainly we must ensure that competencies cannot get up and walk out – leaving us exposed and vulnerable. All this will ensure a greater robustness for our company.

□ Unpuzzling the puzzle of Pieces of Fun

Tom looked round the conference room at the group of people he had invited just two days ago. Everybody was waiting expectantly, wondering what had caused Tom to call this special meeting at such short notice.

"Thank you for coming," Tom said, although he was fully aware that he had given them no choice in the matter. "I've asked you all here today to help me solve a problem."

He noticed the surprised looks pass round the table. Good, he thought. He had got their attention.

"The problem is: how to save Pieces of Fun."

This brought an audible gasp from almost everybody around the table.

"Save Pieces of Fun?" asked Hilary Gregson, the marketing manager. "Save it from what?"

Tom looked at her and wondered how far he should go. To hell with it, he thought, let them have the truth.

"To save Pieces of Fun from closure."

Now the fox was really in the hen-coop. Everybody started talking at once, looks of disbelief on their faces. Tom allowed this for a moment, then held up his hand for silence.

"Ladies and gentlemen," he said, his voice low and confident. "You don't need me to tell you that Pieces of Fun is standing at a crossroads. We have a long history and our financial position at the moment is satisfactory. But we have to acknowledge that we are working in a market which is changing. The market for toys and games is becoming increasingly sophisticated. You know that, Hilary. You've done the market research. We are making money at the moment – but we have no guarantees that we can continue making money in the future."

"I believe you are painting an unnecessarily dismal picture, Tom," said Jeffrey Chambers, the financial director. "Our financial statements are excellent – and I see no cause for such alarm."

"That's true – at least on the surface," said Tom, smiling at his colleague. "The question we have to ask is whether these financial statements give us a full picture of our position – and before you explode, Jeffrey, I'd ask you to hear me out. In fact, I'd like you all to listen for just a few minutes."

He stopped and glanced round the table. He had their attention, he knew, and now he would have to explain everything he had done in the last few days. He picked up the first of a series of overhead sheets he had prepared for this meeting.

"Over the last few weeks, I have been taking a very close look at this company. And I have done this by looking at our core competencies. My analysis has shown that we have three: printing and die-cutting, graphic design, and intellectual entertainment. I have looked at these carefully, and have worked out the value each of these has for our company. In other words, I have tried to show what contribution to profits each of these competencies make. And I can assure you – I was astounded at the results."

He placed the next sheet on the projector.

"As you can see – my calculations show that the present value of each of these competencies is as follows:

- Print and die-cutting – $13.1 million

- Graphic design – $7.4 million

- Intellectual entertainment – $45.5 million."

There were gasps of disbelief around the table.

"Where did those figures come from?" demanded Jeffrey. "I've never seen them before."

"I'm sure you haven't," smiled Tom. "Neither had I. We have been taught to concentrate on tangible assets, on things we can touch. But we have never looked at the intangibles of our company. Things like people, customers, knowledge, experience. They have a value for our company as well. Which is why I've spent a lot of time calculating them. I would ask you all, now, to accept these figures, at least as the basis for our meeting today. Okay?"

There were a few hesitant nods, but nobody spoke.

"I reached these figures by applying five indicators to each competence – indicators for added value, competitiveness, potential, sustainability, and robustness. And this is what revealed a big problem – the one I want you all to help me with today."

He placed another sheet on the projector.

"Our printing and die-cutting competence is the one which has helped make Pieces of Fun the company it is today. I have come to think of it as the heart of the company. It is the competence which is most firmly embedded in our culture. Ask Harry," he added, nodding in the direction of Harry Franklin, the plant manager. "Harry has a lot of highly experienced people in his department, many of them long-standing employees of this company. Their experience and ingenuity has given us a strong position in printing and die-cutting. The problem is that in today's market, this competence – the heart of our company – is making a decreasing contribution to our profits. In fact, by 2002, it will make no contribution whatsoever."

"How can you say that, Tom?" Harry said, unable to contain himself any longer. "We're working full shifts at the moment and we've got orders backed up as it is."

"You're right, Harry," Tom said, understandingly. "But Hilary's market research has shown that the market for puzzles is being eroded. And there's growing competition from Asia. We're very good at what we do – but the question is, whether the market is really interested any more in jigsaw puzzles – even ones from Pieces of Fun."

"So what are you suggesting," demanded Harry. "Do you want to close down the factory? Sell us off?"

"That's the last thing I want to do," said Tom. "Selling off one of our core competencies would mean the death of the company as we know it."

"So what's the alternative?" asked Jeffrey, the financial man.

"That's what I want us to find. That's why I have asked you all here today. To find an alternative."

He held up his hand.

"Let me try to explain. We have a highly developed core competence in printing and die-cutting. That's something we do well. We have developed certain technologies ourselves which give us a lead over the competition. What I want to do is to look at ways in which we can use this competence. Until now we've always placed the competence at the service of our products. Perhaps we should start thinking in a new direction – and define products that we could make using this competence."

He looked round the table and saw that the group he had invited were thinking hard.

"Any idea about new products?"

Harry Franklin, the plant manager, cleared his throat.

"If I understand you correctly, Tom, you want us to forget puzzles for a moment and think about other areas where our competence could be used."

Tom nodded.

"Well," said Harry, taking a deep breath, "if I look at the things we do well, I suppose you could say we could do any sort of printing on paper, cardboard, and plastic. We do that now. And then we do die-cutting. I suppose we could also get into other areas in this field, such as bevel cutting, straight cutting, punching, and perforating. There's a lot of things we could do. We've always developed our technology to meet new needs thought up by the development department, but they've always been directed at puzzles and games. I don't see any reason why our technicians wouldn't be able to develop new techniques in the same field for other applications."

"Any suggestions on applications? Come on – let your minds run away with you. Nothing's too silly at the moment."

"I just bought some mounting sheets for my photo collection. Could we do something like that?" asked Fred O'Leary, head of design.

"Or what about inlays for boxes of soap and perfume," said Hilary.

"Could we get into printing things on unusual shapes – say round or hexagonal, or in the shape of a Roman helmet?" said Alberta Jeffries, head of game development. "Or displays – you know, those big cardboard stand-ups in shops showing Darth Vadar."

"Promotional material sounds a good idea," nodded Hilary. "All sorts of things. Novelty name tags. Flower tags – you know, in special shapes, embossed or whatever you call it. Or Thank you cards. Mail-shots. They're always looking for new ideas. Perhaps we could print mail-shots for a new car, with the mail-shot die cut in the shape of a car. Could we do something like that, Harry?"

"No problem. We can make dies in any shape you like. Don't you remember the round puzzle we produced several years ago – turned out to be a bit of a classic that one. But we can also do perforation. You know   cards for telephone numbers. Reinforced holes, so that they don't tear after a few weeks. That always irritates me, I know. We could make a better job of them than a lot of companies out there."

"Alright," said Tom, after a moment's silence. "You've all come up with a whole lot of ideas about what we can do. But if we are honest, many of these are things we would do in different markets from the traditional ones we have served as Pieces of Fun. All our products are aimed at children and adults who want to entertain themselves. Do you think we should continue concentrating on this group, or should we expand our sights to other people? Can we adapt our present products to other uses and for other people? And if so – who?"

Again he looked round the table expectantly. At first nobody spoke. Then Alberta seemed to have an idea.

"What about the fashion industry? They're always looking for new gimmicks. Perhaps we could make jigsaw jewelry. I don't know – perhaps a jigsaw brooch. It'd have to be made of some high quality material, though. Depends whether we go for the novelty market or the high-end fashion freak."

"I think there are a lot of things we could do with our traditional products to make them more appealing to new groups of people," said Fred, the design chief. "We've already seen how some of our products have become collectors' items. Perhaps we should think of developing collectors' products – plug the nostalgia theme. Make them very up-market. Very high quality. Perhaps on exclusive materials. Or using illustrations commissioned by some of today's leading artists. You know how successful our "Mona Lisa" puzzle was. Imagine what we could do with a whole series of contemporary artists producing a work exclusively for our puzzles."

"Good idea," nodded Hilary, her forehead creased in concentration. "And perhaps we could also accept commissions from companies wanting a special gift. You know the thing – a photograph of the head-office, or a new product, or a new factory. And I think we could also investigate using puzzles as promotional material. We could even develop a puzzle and have a single piece in a bag of crisps, so that people could collect the pieces of the puzzle. Even give a prize to the first person who returns the completed puzzle."

Tom nodded, pleased at the way the session was going. He had never realized that there were so many good ideas in the minds of his people. Perhaps he should hold these sorts of sessions on a more regular basis.

Tony Baker, the sales manager, had been jotting notes on a piece of paper, and now lifted his head to address his colleagues.

"I wonder whether there are uses in the field of education. We all know that puzzles help stimulate the mind. Parents love to give them to their children. Perhaps we should think of developing puzzles specially for babies. Make the pieces from a special product that can be sucked without any harm to the baby or the puzzle. Or perhaps we could think of using puzzles for children – you know, with sums or writing on them. Perhaps use them in the developing countries to help the education drive there. Or we could even use puzzles to help elderly people develop their memories."

Everybody nodded, and Tom brought this part of the discussion to a close.

"I think there are a lot of people who we could approach with adaptations of our existing products. But the final question I would like to ask you is – how? A lot of these ideas don't really fit in to the range offered by our traditional retailers. Yet the retailers have an enormous power. You know the rush we always have towards the end of the third quarter. Retailers put off ordering their Christmas stocks to the very last minute – but expect us to have product ready for them when they order it. The result is that we have to stock-pile product, and that means we carry all the risks – both commercially and financially. They expect us to out-guess them, but they won't leap until the very last minute. And despite this, they still expect us to negotiate discounts, lower prices, and special terms with them. I think we should look at new ways of getting out products to the market. Any ideas?"

"I suppose you're thinking of internet," said Tony Baker. "That's one way of side-stepping the retailers. I suppose we could create a web-site for Pieces of Fun, and offer our products on-line. But I'm not sure whether that would generate large sales on its own."

"Perhaps we should think about creating something, not for ourselves, but for our customers," said John Coleman, head of distribution. "Perhaps a web-site dedicated to puzzle enthusiasts. You know – where they can swap puzzles or offer rare puzzles for sale."

"That could be something," nodded Hilary. "And we could use the site to get feedback on what these enthusiasts want. We could include things like a help line, so give hints about puzzles. Hint books are big business – particularly for cult games. Just look at the books they published for the Larry series of adventure games. They were big sellers."

"You know," said Harry, the plant manager, "perhaps we could even offer an on-line service to people who wanted to create their own puzzles. They could scan in a photograph and send it to us by email, and we could make a one-off puzzle for them. Perhaps we could offer a wedding service or a baby service. You know, a puzzle made of the first picture of a new-born baby to send to all the friends and relatives. Better than a card."

Tom was delighted. He had been given a whole lot of ideas. This was proving a very successful meeting indeed.

⌐ The What, How, Who approach

The approach adopted by Tom Hoffman in his brain-storming session is one which is common enough in today's world. It is known as the "What, How, Who" approach.[1] And it helps people to think out of the box. To break away from traditional ideas and really analyze the problem from a new perspective.

Let us look at how some of today's companies have adopted exactly this approach to help them uncover new possibilities for their existing competencies.

What

On the surface, there is nothing particularly special about baking soda. It is a traditional product, used in bread-making as a leavening agent. Yet with the decline in home bread-making, Arm & Hammer, one of the most important manufacturers of baking soda, saw interest in their product declining. Many managers in the same position would have simply recognized that the product was at the end of its life-cycle, and would have reconciled themselves to a further decline in sales of the product.

But not Arm & Hammer. They decided to see whether this product could be used in other, hitherto non-existent, areas.

Baking soda is a natural product (certainly a pro in today's world), which had a number of interesting properties other than its use as a leavening agent. For example, it is a mild abrasive, making it perfect for cleaning kitchen counters. And many people used it to clean their teeth – it had a natural whitening agent. It is also an anti-acid, and many people had taken it to relieve upset stomachs. It had also been used as a foot-bath, to relieve tired feet, and as a skin lotion, to help relieve rashes. People also discovered that it absorbed undesirable odors, and began placing it in the refrigerators to remove unwanted smells. Others used it on carpets or in cat litter boxes.

A whole range of new product possibilities presented itself – for something which many people had seen as at the end of its life-cycle![2]

Many companies see opportunities in adding services to their existing products. This is particularly true in the volatile world of computers and information technology.

HP has spun-off its medical divisions from its core business of computers and printers, and the new chief executive of the medical business aims to shift the emphasis of the business towards service via internet.

Compaq is aiming to become more than just a manufacturer of successful computers. Instead, its strategy is aimed at becoming a supplier of internet systems and solutions for e-commerce. Recognizing that this will require competencies that they do not have in-house, Compaq has made a series of very successful acquisitions, all aimed at acquiring competencies needed for the new strategy.

Dell has recently started an internet supermarket – Gigabuys.com. This was, perhaps, a logical step for a company which has always led the field in direct mail computer sales. But the competence needed to handle this site has been acquired thanks to an alliance with IBM.

And IBM has returned to its roots: personal computers were always something of a side-line for the company, and it has now decided to concentrate more than ever on service and software.[3]

A good example of finding a new market for an existing technology is shown by a new safety option being introduced on Cadillac's 2000 De Ville. For the first time, drivers will be able to have infrared night-vision technology in their automobile. The technology has been licensed to General Motors by Raytheon Systems Co., which developed the technology which allowed the US Army to spot Iraqi tanks at night during the Gulf War.[4]

Who

Many products are designed with a specific target group in mind – and it only later emerges that it may prove attractive to an alternative group. By addressing the issue of "who," companies can often discover new opportunities for a product which seems to be in decline.

Sam Hornstein, the food broker, created a dog food in the 1990s, which he named "Balto." He had chosen the name to honor a husky that had made headline news by delivering a diphtheria serum to some patients in Alaska. The dog food was marginally successful – he sold around 50,000 cases a year – but he started getting complaints about the high fish content of his food. This may have been perfect for a dog such as Balto the husky – it proved too rich for less active animals.

Hornstein was faced with a decision: revise the formula to satisfy a more average dog, or look for an alternative "who."

It was the smell of fish which gave the answer: he continued marketing the same recipe, but now under the name "Puss 'n' Boots" and discovered that cats loved his food. Hornstein eventually sold his successful cat-food business to Quaker Oats Inc. for $6 million.[5]

At first glance, you would think that technologies developed for the Nuclear Power industry would have few applications in other fields. But the reverse is true.

One nuclear power station was looking for new applications for its proprietary technology – a switch which allows an almost instant shut-down of the reactor in an emergency. They eventually found a new market: as a safety switch for amusement park rides![6]

How

Of all the innovations of the 20th century, the automated car production line, first introduced by Henry Ford in the 1920s, has seemed to weather the storms of change with consummate ease. The original campaign developed for the T Ford – "You can have it in any color as long as it's black" – demonstrates, perhaps more clearly than anything else, how the automotive industry has always been, essentially, a seller's market. The traditional production line – designed to mass-produce products of identical or very similar specifications – has always been the backbone of the industry.

But today, those massive, traditional production lines are under threat. Not least because the automotive industry is no longer a seller's market – it is a buyer's market.

Throughout society there is a strong trend towards individuality. The fashion industry no longer issues an annual decree that the hemline will be x inches above or below the knee. Instead, there is a fragmentation, in which trends – and increasingly there are a wide range of trends – are set down with broad strokes of the brush, leaving the details to the taste and style of the individual. Mix and match has become the key phrase.

The same trend is very true in the automotive industry. In the race to appeal to customers, car manufacturers are offering more opportunities for customization than ever before. Body types, engine sizes, colors, interiors, accessories – all give the customer the chance to design his or her ideal car. Compact? Sporty? Family? Town car? Touring car? Off the road? The choice is yours.

What's more, the number of add-ons offered to customers – add-ons, incidentally, which also help automobile manufacturers differentiate their product from that of the competition – are proliferating. And the result is that niche markets are now emerging. Ford and Audi are developing aluminum cars, which have exceptionally low gas emissions, thus helping to combat the greenhouse effect. High-end cars are being fitted with an ever-increasing range of options: the navigation systems in Volvo, BMW, and Mercedes or the night vision system in the Cadillac from General Motors. And soon governmental regulations will also require new add-ons, as electronic toll systems come into effect.

With the growth in choice, many automobile companies are choosing new ways of attracting customers. There are indications that the whole sales process is becoming as direct as that pioneered by Dell. Ford has joined up with Microsoft to sell their cars on-line. It will offer the customer the chance to buy a "built-to-order" car – and have it delivered faster than ever before. All options – such as color, interior, trim, accessories, and so on – can be viewed and chosen on-line, and the final car delivered in a matter of days, instead of the weeks and months which have been common until now. General Motors, not wishing to be left behind, has entered into an alliance with Sun Microsystems. And Toyota is now guaranteeing delivery of the finished car within five days – a time-to-market which is setting a new standard for the industry.

But still the automotive industry is faced with a conundrum: how to produce customized cars, in an ever smaller series, on a production line designed to mass manufacture essentially identical products. Many automotive companies have been addressing this problem. BMW, for example, has developed a JIT production line, on which it can produce all its models, in any variation, in any order. A specific car can be tracked for production date, specifications, and so on.

The new on-line ordering systems will force manufacturers to streamline their supply chain management and rapid production of a specific vehicle will become more important than mass production of largely identical products.[7]

Much of the activities in the automotive industry seem to follow the advice of K. Kelly: "Don't solve problems, pursue opportunities."[8] And Ford is an example of just how many opportunities there are out there.

Ford, once the very symbol of mass-production, is today moving away from concentrating on the end product, preferring to reshape its business to offer its customers an experience. This requires a radical change of direction. Ford's component business is now being concentrated in a separate company – Visteon – which may very well be spun-off when the time is right. The company is also making more extensive use of sub-contractors, rather than manufacturing everything in house. At the same time, Ford is acquiring additional service companies. It has taken over KwikFit in Europe, a company which offers instant exhaust and tire replacement. It has also acquired a car recycling business in the States, and the consumer-arm of Mazda in Japan. It is even offering its dealers a satellite feed service for audio and other activities, at a monthly fee. All this, plus its huge financing operation and its car rental business, Hertz.

All this comes back to the fact we mentioned earlier: the service industry cannot exist without factories, and factories cannot exist without the service industry. Car manufacturers are happy to generate margins of 5% for their vehicles; margins from financing and ancillary industries can be as high as 10 to 15%. Ford's top man, Jacques Nasser, believes that Ford must become much more than an automobile giant. The sale of a car is no longer the end of the cycle, but the beginning. Financing, servicing, accessories, maintenance, car rental, leasing, and insurance all follow the sale. And these are the areas that generate higher margins. Don Hume, the communications director, explains the tactics: "We are developing into a world-wide company special-izing in mobility." You will notice that the word "automobile" is no longer mentioned by Ford![9]

⌐ Out of the box

Tom looked round at his staff again, and pulled out a new sheet. He placed it on the projector and turned to the table.

"We've looked at our competencies and come up with a whole lot of new ideas for exploiting them more efficiently. But that is just the start. I want us all now to think out of the box – come up with … well – just about anything. I've written down a number of areas that we should look at. The first is our sales pattern. We're trapped in the seasonal buying cycle. More than 40% of our sales are generated in the fourth quarter of the year. And you all know the difficulties this creates. Let's all think about new opportunities for moving our product. Any ideas?"

For a moment nobody spoke, as they all thought about the situation. Then Hilary raised her head and looked round the table.

"We know that a lot of people buy our puzzles as presents. But it seems that we think that means Christmas. There are other times people need presents. Perhaps we should ask ourselves when."

The others nodded and all began speaking at once. Tom held up his hand and asked for them to speak one at a time, so that he could take notes.

"Birthdays," said Harry.

"But that's an existing market, I would have thought," said Hilary. "I was thinking more of things like Mother's Day."

"You mean developing a special Mother's Day puzzle?" asked Fred.

"Perhaps. A jigsaw puzzle of a bunch of flowers instead of the flowers themselves."

"Or customized puzzles – you know, with a special message: 'To the best mother in the world from Tom, Dick, or Harry,'" said Alberta. "We could take orders on them in advance and ship them direct to the address."

"And we could do the same for Father's Day," added Hilary.

"And even for birthdays," said Harry, a smile on his face. "We could offer a service to make a puzzle of a photograph of the birthday boy or girl, man or woman. Personalization. Must be a market for that."

"And what about Valentine's Day," John Coleman. "Lots of spending done then. A heart-shaped puzzle with a photograph of your loved one on it. With a special message."

"Or an American flag for the Fourth of July."

"Or a Halloween puzzle."

"But what about our board games?" asked Alberta. "We could think of special games for Thanksgiving. That's as much a family affair as Christmas."

Tom nodded, again pleased at the suggestions which he had heard.

"You've come up with some good ideas. Ideas that can help reduce our dependency on a traditional period. Spread our sales more evenly. I think we should look into them. Let's leave this for now and look at my second point. You all know that I'm relatively new to this business. But it still seems to me that we are stuck in our ways. We continue doing things in the same way – and accepting the norms of the products we produce. Can we do anything with our products which the rest of the industry don't do?"

"Can you give us an idea of your thinking," asked Hilary, after a moment's silence.

Tom thought for a moment, then smiled.

"So you want me to do the work for you, do you," he laughed. "Let me see. I suppose what I mean is adapting the ideas of the puzzle to new technology. Make the puzzle a new challenge. The thing is, the puzzles we make at the moment stay the same. Once you've done one – that's it. Okay – we make puzzles with a large number of pieces – but they all stay the same. And it gets easier to do them a second time."

"That's good," said Tony, the sales manager. "Means people buy new puzzles when they want a new challenge."

"I suppose so. But just imagine that we could market a puzzle that had pieces that changed shape."

"Oh, come on," said Harry, a look of total disbelief on his face. "How do you expect us to do that? Supply the buyer with a magic wand?"

"Good idea," said Tom, a smile on his face. "But not very believable. No – I was thinking more in the lines of an electronic puzzle. You could have the pieces on a screen, and if you take too long to finish the puzzle, then the pieces you've already placed can gradually change shape."

"Mind-boggling," said Alberta, a look of wonder on her face. "That would mean you would have to set a time limit – perhaps an electronic egg-timer. Give an additional challenge – a sort of race against the clock. I like it."

"Well," said Fred, the head of design, "that's one idea. But if we're thinking in virtual games – because that's what your idea is all about – then why stick to 2-D pieces. We could have a three-dimensional game, which would work just the same. The pieces could then be any shape and size we wanted – because there would be no need to make them. I think that's the way the market is going."

"But we shouldn't forget our strength," said Harry, a worried frown crossing his brow. "I mean, we're good at making physical puzzles."

"And we will continue doing that," said Tom. "We've come up with lots of ideas for using our traditional competencies. Now we're expanding another of them: our ability to provide intellectual entertainment. That's where electronics come in, I think. Agreed?"

The people round the table nodded, even Harry. Tom smiled again, and decided to move on.

"You know, this brings me to my next point: What can we do to raise our standards above those in the industry? What ideas can we generate for adding new services? Let me give you an idea.

"When I was a young kid, I had a puzzle that I loved. You know – one of those puzzles with jumbo pieces, specially for children."

"We still make those now," said Harry, nodding round the table.

"I used to do that puzzle every day. It had a picture of Mickey Mouse – and I loved it. But then, one day, one of the pieces disappeared. I don't know how that happened – but in a house with four children, we got used to things going missing. I cried for days. Eventually my mother went out and found a replacement puzzle. Had to pay the full amount for it.

"I started thinking of that when I was preparing for this meeting. Perhaps we could offer a replacement service for individual pieces. What do you think?"

"I think it's a good idea," said Harry, "but it would be difficult. How would a customer order a particular piece? We'd have to print some sort of guide for them. It would be difficult – but I suppose it could be done."

"Perhaps we could put that on a website. We've talked about websites today – we could put our puzzles on the website with codes on each piece."

"And we could even offer tips and clues via the website," said Hilary. "After all, our games and puzzles are supposed to challenge people. If they get stuck, they often give up. We could give them hints on how to proceed. Nobody else in the industry does that."

"That's what we need," said Tom. "To do things that nobody else in the industry is doing. And I think we can also do this by raising standards. Any ideas?"

"Do you mean quality," asked Jeffrey. "We already offer high quality in our products."

"That's true – but could we offer even higher standards? Really go for the top end of the market."

"A sort of fashion house?" asked Hilary.

"Why not?" said Harry. "We can print to higher standards than we do today. It's a question of whether the market would be prepared to pay."

"I think they might be – if we kept them exclusive," said Tony. "But then I think we'd have to find alternative sales outlets. You don't go into a toy shop for an exclusive present."

"You're right," said John Coleman, the distribution manager. "But you mustn't forget that that's where we do most of our business. It'll take time to get our products into new outlets. But it could be done. We'd have to target boutiques and department stores."

"Or offer them on-line," said Hilary. "Perhaps we should offer exclusive puzzles exclusively on-line. A sort of top of the range idea."

"It's worth thinking about," said Tom.

"You know what," he added. "I think it's time for a coffee break. Agreed?"

⊡ Are you ready to break through traditional boundaries?

No matter how hard we try, we all get trapped within conventional boundaries. "Caught in the box."

Yet that is exactly what we must avoid. In a world of change, we can no longer accept traditional boundaries and abide by them. We must be prepared to break them down.

In their article "Creating new market space,"[10] W. Chan Kim and Renée Mauborgne offer a guideline for managers wishing to look beyond the conventionally defined boundaries of competition. They suggest that managers ask themselves four questions:

- *Reduce:* What factors can be reduced well below the industry standard?

- *Create:* What factors can be created that the industry has never offered?

- *Raise:* What factors should be raised well beyond the industry standard?

- *Eliminate:* What factors should be eliminated that the industry has taken for granted?

When Tom asked this question, he concentrated on reducing the traditional peak period in his sales cycle. It was certainly something which affects the whole toy industry – but this doesn't mean it should be accepted. Tom's team came up with a whole range of ideas for developing markets in times when toys and puzzles were not traditionally sold.

All too often, companies confine their analysis to their own market segment. But Kim and Mauborgne feel that considerable insight can be gained by looking at what they call "substitute" industries. After all, they maintain, a company does not only compete with companies in its own sector, but also with companies in other industries, offering substitute or ancillary services and products.

As a consumer, we make a whole lot of decisions about "substitute" services almost automatically. Say we have decided on an evening out. Do we choose a film? A show? A game? Dinner? A disco? A concert? Ballet? Opera? All of these are substitute services. Of course, if we decide to take in a show, then we have a choice within the sector. But even that's not the end to it. Because we still have to decide how to get there – car, train, bus, taxi, limousine.

These sort of decisions, Kim and Mauborgne, say, are made automatically. We accept the substitutes and choose between them.

The trouble is – we don't do this in our businesses. If we own a cinema, then we look at the other films being shown – and design our competitive strategy to gain an advantage over those competitors. We forget – or so it would seem – the substitutes, such as theater, games, or whatever. We create compartments – and stay in our boxes.

Successful companies have frequently found ways of breaking out of "traditional" compartments. One such company, described in the article by Kim and Mauborgne, is Home Depot.

Over the last 20 years, the do-it-yourself company has grown to reach a projected 1,100 stores throughout North America by the end of 2000 – and has revolutionized the industry on the way. It has achieved this success not by taking away market share from other hardware stores; it has done it by getting out of the box it found itself in.

One of the key factors to Home Depot's success was that it understood the concept of substitute markets. People, they reasoned, who were interested in home improvements could choose one of two options: they could hire a contractor; or they could do it themselves.

Home Deport asked themselves why a home owner would choose a contractor – even though hiring one still required a considerable amount of time and attention from the customer while the job was being done. And the answer, they realized, was because the contractor had specialized know-how which the home owner lacks. And looking at the matter from the other side, Home Deport asked why, then, did so many home owners decide to do it themselves? And the answer was, obviously, to save money.

This led to a two-pronged approach. First, Home Depot made it their job to help the confidence of home-owners. This they did by employing staff with practical experience in contracting work – often carpenters and painters – who were able to give first-time do-it-yourselfers helpful tips and practical information. They would discuss the whole project with the customer, walking them through each part of the process and pointing out particular areas of attention. In addition, Home Depot sponsored a large number of in-store clinics, dealing with technical matters such as electrical wiring, plumbing, and so on.

Second, Home Depot looked at ways to cut prices to their minimum. Typical hardware stores had a lot of frills and extras which simply bumped up the prices. Home Depot was convinced that the do-it-yourselfer on a tight budget was prepared to do without all these extras, such as central (high-priced) city locations and attractive display shelves.

Home Depot's success formula combines the attractiveness of two substitute industries: they offer the expertise of a home contractor, but prices which are much lower than traditional hardware stores. It really is a matter of killing two birds with one stone.

◳ Who is the customer?

The group of Pieces of Fun experts had returned from their short break. And when they all arrived in the meeting room, they saw that Tom had put up a new sheet. It read, quite simply, "Who is our customer?"

When they had all taken their seats, Tom looked round expectantly. At first nobody spoke, so Tom asked the question out loud: "I want you to tell me who is our customer."

"The person who plays our games and does our puzzles?" asked Alberta.

"The person who buys them?" asked Tony.

"So which is it?" asked Tom. "The buyer or the user?"

It was Hilary who broke the silence.

"I suppose it's both. Parents usually buy puzzles for their children, and often look for something which they think will appeal to them. On the other hand, it's ultimately the children who play the games – and if it sucks, they'll forget about it."

"I think they'd do more than that," said Tom. "I think they'd tell their friends how bad the game is. Then their friends would tell their parents not to buy that game. On the other hand, if a game's good, then the word gets round and children start asking for it.

"I've thought about this for a long time, and I think there are three groups we have as customers: users, purchasers, and influencers. We have to make sure we appeal to all these groups. The question is – how?"

"I suppose for the user and influencer, you need to create a hype. You know – the way they do with Star Wars or whatever."

"But will the hype appeal to the parents – the purchasers?" asked Tom.

"Not necessarily," answered Alberta. "I think we all know that parents like to think they are buying something educational for their children. The learn as you play idea. So it means combining the hype with an educational aspect. It's the combination of the two which is important. They have to be in balance, otherwise the product won't appeal to anybody. So maybe we can create a hype around a new cartoon character and make sure that at the same time the games in which this character plays an important role are educational as well. Then we have a product that suits the buyer, the user and the influencer as well."

The chain of buyers

Even in today's highly diversified world, companies still like to put their customers into tiny pigeon-holes. Even those companies which proclaim most loudly that they are "customer-oriented" often direct their attention at a single target customer, even though – as Tom found out in his brain-storming session – there is frequently a chain of buyers, each making their own evaluation of and decision on a product. The "buyer" is not necessarily the "user" – and they may both be swayed in their decision by an "influencer." These groups may overlap – in that they are all interested in the same product – but they often differ, in that they each have their own priorities when judging a product or service.

The fashion industry shows how each of the various groups must be taken into consideration. The large season collection shows are not aimed at the "user" – but rather at the "influencers" – fashion editors and commentators – and the "buyers" – in this case, the buyers for large, influential retail outlets. The users will ultimately choose what the influencers recommend and what the buyers offer in their outlets. Yet the fashion industry also appeals directly to the user: not only does it run advertisements with photographs of its collections, it also has boutiques that are aimed directly at the user – frequently with a selection which is exclusive to these outlets.

Many large companies have found it convenient to target "buyers" as their major target group – frequently corporate purchasing departments. This is true of such industries as office equipment and automation and IT systems. Often these are designed to "make life easy" for the purchaser, rather than the user.

This was certainly the case in the world of business information providers. Until the 1990s, the world of on-line financial information provision was dominated by two players: Reuters and Telerate. They both offered integrated systems which appealed to IT managers – the buyers – who preferred standardized systems, since this greatly eased their work.

Bloomberg entered the market with a totally different slant on what was required. It was the traders and dealers, Bloomberg reasoned, that made the money – not the IT managers. But the systems provided did little to help them make the sort of split-second decisions which can make or break a deal. And so they designed a system which took the needs of the user into account, rather than the needs of the buyer. The system includes two screens, allowing access to a wide range of data without having to open windows for specific information. The keyboards were equipped with keys with clear indications of specific financial information, so that users could have information completely at their finger-tips. Bloomberg also realized that decisions were often based on "what if" scenarios – so the possibility of running these was included in the system. Previously the trader would have to download information and make calculations using notepads and calculators; now they do it directly on-line.

Having defined their target group as the users, Bloomberg went even further. They analyzed the traders and found that the group earned very high salaries, but their long working hours gave them little chance of spending their money. Bloomberg discovered that there were slow times when there was little activity in the market – and therefore for the traders. And so they included a system which allowed traders to purchase items such as flowers, clothing, travel, theater tickets, and presents on-line.

By shifting its focus from the traditional "buyer" to the "user," Bloomberg has now become an important force in the financial information market.

Philips Lighting Company, the North American division of Dutch-based Royal Philips Electronics, had traditionally competed in a market which concentrated on corporate purchasers. These were interested in two matters: the cost of the electric light bulb and its life. Everybody in the lighting industry were forced to compete in these two areas.

Philips Lighting Company took a long look at the total market, and discovered that there were hidden costs involved, due to environmentally toxic mercury which these lamps contained. Companies faced high disposal costs for the lamps at the end of their lives – something which was unknown to the purchasing department, but well-known to the CFOs.

Philips decided to address this problem and developed an environmentally friendly bulb which it promoted directly with the CFOs, using the influencers to drive the sales. The Alto has reduced overall company costs and has earned Philips very good press as an environmentally friendly company. What's more, the new market in which Alto operated had higher margins and the product has already replaced more than 25% of the traditional fluorescent lamps used in offices, schools, and stores throughout the States.

All this shows that it is important to understand the chain of buyers in your business. By carefully analyzing the needs of each group – users, buyers, and influencers – it is possible to create a totally new market, with all the benefits that implies.[11]

Do puzzles exist in a world of their own?

Tom turned to the group assembled in the meeting room. Time to move on.

"We've looked at the chain of buyers – and now I'd like to ask another question. Are there any things which influence our puzzles – things which we have no control over?"

"Can you explain that to me?" asked Harry, scratching his head.

"Well, Harry. How often do you go to the cinema?"

"Not as often as I did when I was young."

"Why?"

"Well – we'd like to. My wife loves the cinema. But it's such a hassle. We have to find a sitter and leave enough time to park the car. It all becomes something like a military operation."

Tom nodded.

"Exactly. If you run a cinema, you have to be aware of the other things which can influence attendance. It's not just the film or the price of the ticket – it's the other things, like hiring a sitter and parking the car. What I want to know is whether there are those sorts of things surrounding our puzzles."

"It's funny, you know," smiled Hilary. "I have a friend who always loved doing puzzles. The bigger and more complicated the better. She had a special room for herself – with a big table in it where she could spread out the pieces. But then she became pregnant for the third time and had to turn the room into a nursery. I gave her our latest puzzle for her last birthday – you know, the one with 7,500 pieces – and she said: 'This is great. But I don't have the room to do it anymore. I can't use the dining table, because I could never finish a puzzle of this size in one day. And we need the table in the evening for dinner with the family. And they use the table for homework and things like that. There's just no room for me and my puzzles.' Could we do anything about that?"

"You mean like go onto the real estate market and build houses with special puzzle rooms," grinned Fred.

"I wasn't thinking of anything quite as drastic as that," quipped Tom with a smile. "But I think there's something in what Hilary tells. Big puzzles require a lot of space. And today, people often don't have it. Can we think of anything creative?"

"I think the problem lies in the very nature of puzzles," said Alberta. "Enthusiasts often have the idea 'the bigger the better.' So you need a very big flat surface to do them on. And that means you can't use that surface for anything else. And the surface has to be horizontal, otherwise the pieces fall all over the place."

"Isn't there any way to let people store their puzzles while they're doing them?" asked Tony. "I mean, a vertical board could be stored behind a cupboard or sofa. It wouldn't get in the way."

"But how can you store a puzzle vertically?" asked John. "The pieces would fall everywhere."

"Could we make magnetic puzzles?" asked Harry. "A metal board, with magnetic pieces, so that they wouldn't fall off when the board is stored upright."

"That would be good for a new product," nodded Tom, "but it doesn't solve the problem for our existing range."

"But we could create a special puzzle board," said Hilary. "It could have a flap which comes over the puzzle and locks in place, keeping the pieces you've finished as they were. We could market that as a unique item."

"And I wouldn't be surprised if the sales of puzzles were stimulated by it," said Jeffrey. "There must be thousands of people like your friend who have given up doing puzzles because there is no place to store them. I like the idea."

⊔ Thinking of complementary services

It is all too easy to see your activities in a narrow confine. To forget matters which could have a decisive effect on whether your product or service is successful. Matters which, all too often, fall outside your direct field of influence. Cinema owners, after all, can do little about the need for baby-sitters or parking. Unless they develop a children's nursery and build their own parking lots.

The problem is, however, that many of us recognize the influence such external factors have on our business. Of course we talk about seasonal demand. About competitors. But these are, once again, focussed at our specific product and service. What we really have to ask ourselves is: what happens before, during, and after our product or service is used? Restaurants should not only ensure that a dining experience is excellent – it should also recognize that guests will have to get to and from the restaurant, and should never be surprised when somebody asks them to "call me a cab".

According to Kim and Mauborgne,[12] "companies can create new market space by zeroing in on the complements that detract from the value of their own product or service." They then cite the case of Borders and B&N, two booksellers which discovered that it was possible – and profitable – to do more than just sell books.

Traditionally, a bookshop is a place where people go to buy books – they enter, make their choice, pay, and leave. That's it. But it was obviously not working, but book sales were dropping significantly. Most booksellers blamed the drop in sales in the public's growing indifference to reading. But Borders and B&N decided to look beyond the simple sales moment: they tried to understand the total experience a person is looking for when buying a book. They focussed eventually on the joy of life-long learning and discovery. This did, of course, involve the purchase of a book – but it also involved hunting and searching, evaluating potential purchases, and actually sampling books.

Most book shops catered to an "informed" public – people who knew which book they wanted and bought it. As a result, the sales staff were trained as cashiers and stock clerks – ask them about a book and they had little idea. What's more, stores discouraged browsing, thus placing the responsibility for a purchase fully with the buyer. Nor was the stock held sufficient to cater to all tastes. It was not, to be perfectly honest, a total experience.

Borders and B&N changed all that. They created a new format of super-stores which opened up the industry. Wherever either of the companies opened a new store, the overall consumption of books in that area increases by anything up to 50%. The reason is that these superstores offer a total experience. Customers are encouraged to browse – the superstores are furnished with armchairs, reading-tables, and sofas, and customers can stay and read as long as they like. This experience is further enhanced by coffee bars, classical music, and hired staff who are genuinely interested in books. What's more, the stores stay open until 11 at night, so that people can enjoy an evening's read if they so choose.

This approach has radically changed the image of bookstores. No longer do people feel as if they are obliged to purchase as quickly as possible, but rather that they can enjoy a total reading experience, in which they can investigate and search, and even read, before they actually buy. Today,

Borders and B&N are the two largest book-selling chains in the States, with more than 650 superstores between them.[13]

⌐ Puzzled by emotion

Tom looked round again. He had reached the last point he wanted to discuss with the people here. And he knew it was an important point.

"We've come to the last point I want to discuss with you," he said, "and that's how we can add emotion to our products. I think there's an opportunity for us out there, even with our traditional products. There is a growing number of elderly people, and they could form a very interesting market for us. They have been brought up with puzzles, they enjoy doing them, and now they have sufficient time for such pastimes. But I think we need to appeal emotionally to them. So I want to ask you for some ideas about this – and whether you think this is an interesting market for us or not."

Everybody nodded, but it was Tony who spoke.

"I think we forget about this group too much. We concentrate our sales in toyshops, and not many elderly people go into those, except when buying a present for the grandchildren. Could we make use of these same outlets for elderly people? Perhaps when children want to buy a present for their grandparents …?"

"I certainly think the distribution aspect will have to be investigated," said Tom. "But let me ask you another question: do our products *as they are* appeal to elderly people?"

"I suppose our Great Masters series would," said Harry. "And our floral arrangements. I think we originally designed those for an older market."

"That's true," nodded Alberta. "But if you want new ideas … What about old photographs of cities. You know – remember Chicago when you lived there as a child. Things like that."

"That's good," nodded Hilary. "Nostalgia always sells to elderly people."

"Or their family," said Jeffrey. "We mentioned making customized puzzles for a variety of occasions. What about customized photographs of families – you know, son and daughter and the grandchildren. I think elderly people would like something like that."

"What about packaging?" asked John. "Couldn't we do something with that? I mean, if we're talking nostalgia – then let's go for it. Create a series which is out and out nostalgia. Sort of 'remember the old days when you gathered round the fire and enjoyed yourselves.' Could even call the series: 'Puzzles for long winter evenings.' Something like that, anyway."

"That would go down well with this target group," said Hilary. "We have to give the products some sort of added value. Take it out of the children's area. Take it up-market. I think we have to remember that puzzles are often gifts – so you want that gift to be special, particularly for your parents or grandparents. Perhaps we should create a really deluxe edition – something like Super Gold, or Collector Series. Something which would add value to the puzzle – no matter what we actually decide to put on it."

Tom seemed pleased. Again his people had shown that they had a lot of ideas. It was now time to bring the meeting to a close.

"Well – everybody. I'm impressed. I never realized how many ideas there were in the company. Thank you for your efforts. And let's make a go of Pieces of Fun."

To his surprise, everybody started to clap. And that simple gesture only strengthened his determination to make Pieces of Fun the best in the business.

⊔ Add emotion to products, add functionality to emotions

Understanding that both emotions and functionality play an important role in any buying decision is essential to today's business manager. Yet many companies concentrate on one or other of these aspects. There are some businesses which compete purely on price and function; others concentrate solely on creating an emotional response to their products. Yet it is becoming ever clearer than this is not a clear cut "either/or" situation; it is once again an "and/and" decision. The problem is, that many companies which are functionally oriented, become more so as time goes by – and the same is true of emotionally oriented companies. Both move farther along a path which they have followed slavishly throughout their history.

The problem is that the attitudes of the companies ultimately condition the reflexes of their customers. Functionality? Then that's what customers come to expect. Emotions? Then give us more of the same. And these attitudes are confirmed by market research, which then becomes ammunition for a company to continue in exactly the same way it has always done.

"Companies often find new market space when they are willing to challenge the functional-emotional orientation of their industry. We have observed two common patterns. Emotionally-oriented industries offer many extras that add price without enhancing functionality. Stripping those extras away may create a fundamentally simpler, lower-priced, lower-cost business model that customers would welcome. Conversely, functionally-oriented industries can often infuse commodity products with new life by adding a dose of emotion – and in so doing, can stimulate new demand."[14]

One very good example of how a functional product can be transformed into an emotional one is the success of Starbucks, the chain of coffee shops which has revolutionized the way Americans consider coffee.

Until Starbucks entered the market, coffee was considered little more than a commodity product. Americans drank it everyday – but that's about as far as it went. The industry had led the consumer to believe that they should make their choice based on price, discount coupons, and brand names. The existing companies – the giants General Foods, Nestlé, and Procter & Gamble – sold coffee by the can; Starbucks introduced a retailing coffee shop concept, which many consumers came to refer to as a "caffeine-induced oasis." Starbucks bars offered coffee – but also became chic meeting places, offering status, conversation, and creative coffee drinks. Coffee became an emotional experience. And consumers seemed willing to pay $3 a cup for the Starbucks concept.

Another area where emotion was introduced into a traditionally functionally-oriented product was that of low-prices watches. Low-price watches were originally intended to do little more than tell the time. True the two market leaders – Citizen and Seiko – competed with technology (quartz, digital displays, and so on), but this only reinforced the product's functional image.

And then Swatch came on the market. The Swiss parent company, SMH, set up a design center in Italy to come up with watches which would make a fashion statement. And this has transformed the market. Whereas traditionally consumers would buy one low-price watch, they now, in Italy, own on average six Swatches, choosing the one to wear to match their clothing.

The Body Shop took the opposite approach – moving the traditionally emotional cosmetic products into a functional area.

On average, a top cosmetic brand will spend up to 85% of the retail price on packaging and advertising. Strip this away, The Body Shop calculated, and you could make dramatic savings. Rather than offering its products in stylish glass bottles – which add nothing to the products' functionality – The Body Shop sells its products in refillable plastic bottles. Advertising has been cut to a minimum, since this also adds little if anything to the functionality. The result? Consumers chose The Body Shop for common sense reasons, rather than emotional ones.[15]

Decision time for Tom

Back in his office, Tom Hoffman reviewed the results of his brain-storming session. There were lots of good and fresh ideas. He was pleased. Yet many of the ideas involved radical departures from the traditional way of doing things, and Tom wondered very seriously whether Pieces of Fun could undertake these things on their own.

He looked through his notes and realized that much of what had been discussed revolved around developing new distribution systems. Web-pages, Hint sites, direct-order customized puzzles. All these things required distribution systems which were foreign to the company. Would they be able to create new distribution systems on their own?

The same worry bothered him about entering more firmly the games market. Could they really go up against the Nintendos, Segas, and Sonys of this world? Or could they go head to head with some of the giant publishing companies which were active in the field?

He thought about this for a while, then decided that he would have to investigate the possibility of acquiring competencies which he did not already have. He thought about possible joint ventures. This could get him the competencies he would need in the future. This was something which he would have to think about further. And look around to see whether there were any potential candidates which could offer the competence which he felt his company needed.

Combine existing competencies with newly acquired ones

No company lives in a vacuum. Yet many operate as if they do. And in today's rapidly changing market, that can often spell disaster.

Forward-looking companies are recognizing that strength can be found in acquisitions and mergers, particularly with companies which offer complementary competencies needed for success in changing markets. Mega-mergers, such as the recent one between America Online and Time Warner, show how complementary competencies are being sought to ensure a dominant presence on the internet. And in England, Richard Branson's Virgin has entered into a joint venture with Microsoft in its bid to run the UK National Lottery.

The question which arises, however, is why some mergers are greeted enthusiastically by the market – with shares in the companies concerned increasing – while others are frowned upon – resulting in drops in share prices. And the answer to this can, perhaps, best be sought in whether the market perceives that there is a synergy between the companies, whether the competencies each has are complementary, and whether the value of the whole is more than the sum of the parts.

Certainly, mergers, acquisitions, and joint ventures which are undertaken to acquire complementary competencies are the ones most likely to succeed – not only on the stock exchange, but also in the market-place.

Take the case of the National Australia Bank's acquisition of Florida mortgage lender HomeSide. HomeSide rightly boasted a highly efficient mortgage process, and National Australia Bank plans to transfer this process to its banks in Australia, New Zealand, and the United Kingdom. ABN AMRO, the Dutch-based world bank, also acquired a mortgage lender – the American Standard & Federal. This acquisition resulted in both cost savings and process improvement: Standard & Federal's mortgage operations were so efficient that it now handles all the mortgage business of the combined banks.

Speed to market is often a driver for acquisitions. It was exactly this which encouraged Johnson Controls to acquire Prince Corporation – a specialist industry producing various parts for the automobile industry. Prince Corporate clearly led Johnson Controls in two vital areas: the ability to understand the needs of automobilists, and produce products which satisfied their needs and enjoyed higher margins, and the ability to ramp up production at approximately twice the speed of Johnson Controls. Thanks to the acquired expertise, Johnson Control has been able to improve both its speed to market and its margins.

Gannet is a major newspaper publisher, with some 85 newspapers. It has an enormous database, in which financial and non-financial measures for each of the newspapers is stored. Executives use this database to define best practices. These in turn allow revenue improvement and cost reduction. Every newspaper acquired by Gannet has shown a noticeable improvement in its operations. In fact, thanks to a more efficient production and distribution process, deadlines for news and advertising copy have been reduced, while distribution is faster than ever. [16]

To patent or not

Tom looked down the list of suggestions which had been made. There was a lot there, but he knew that alternatives existed. He knew that some companies were able to make a lot of money by patenting certain aspects of their core competencies and then enjoy income from those patents.

Would this idea work for Pieces of Fun?

He thought long and hard. The one competence which had a high technological component was printing and die-cutting. Certainly there were several areas in which his company had developed important improvements. But in today's highly competitive market, he knew that most of his competitors in this specific competence had already caught up. There was nothing really revolutionary – or unique – which he felt could be patented. It was a pity, because he was convinced this could have offered a solution to some of his problems.

He then looked at the other two competencies. Intellectual entertainment? Nothing to patent there. And graphic design? He supposed that there were companies which were far more advanced in this field than Pieces of Fun were. No patents.

⌐ Search for hidden patent potential

Many companies have discovered that a core competence can provide no new opportunities. It is as if it is destined to do what they have always done. Yet this is no reason to think they are at the end of their usefulness. Certainly in today's highly technical word, there may be certain elements of your competence which gives it a lead over the rest of the industry. Perhaps it is an improvement of a loading mechanism. The use of a special material preparation process. A certain distribution feature.

If you can truly find no new way to leverage your competence – and this can frequently happen as the competence matures – then all is not lost: you can still exploit your competencies by looking for patenting possibilities.

Patents – and the income a company can enjoy from patent licensing fees – have become an increasingly desirable element in a company's portfolio. Examples are about of companies enjoying enormous profits over a long period of time thanks to patents. JVC, for example, still enjoys licensing profits from its various patents on its VHS video system. While Philips and Sony share profits from patents on the CD.

In a publication entitled "Patent Intelligence & Technology Report," a list was published of the top 25 companies according to patent ownership. Top of the list which reads like a Who's Who of modern industry was IBM, with 1,742 patents registered in its name. It was followed by companies such as

Canon, NEC, Motorola, Mitsubishi, Hitachi, Fujitsu, Toshiba, Sony, and Eastman Kodak, all with more than 750 patents apiece.

Yet before you get the idea that patents is something for the giants – the report mentioned a notable trend: there is an increasing number of small companies making patent applications in the US.[17]

IBM has been top of the list for five straight years. Yet it was not always so eager to pursue patents. In 1990, the company earned just $30 million in patent licensing rights. But it was at that time, too, that a growing awareness of the value of intellectual property began seeping through the organization. This led to an aggressive policy of patent application – and today the company's income from its patents has increased an incredible 3,300% over 1990 to more than $1 billion today.[18]

Patents, of course, have not only been the source of income; they have also been a way of protecting a market. For many years, Xerox, thanks to its seminal xerography patents enjoyed a legal monopoly of the copying market. When Xerox was eventually forced by court ruling to license these patents, the company sold its domination of the market decrease rapidly, and with it its earnings and profits.[19]

It would be tempting to think that patents are something which can only apply to technical processes and technological inventions. And this thinking would mean that the days of patents – now that we are moving into a market where innovative ways of doing business give a company its competitive advantage much more than products and services – are numbered. Nothing, however, could be farther from the truth. Dell has secured 42 patents – both issued and pending – on its innovative business model. The patents cover not only Dell's customer configurable on-line ordering system but also the ways in which this is integrated into the company's "continuous flow" manufacturing and delivery process.[20]

The possession of these patents could traditionally – cf. Xerox – have safeguarded Dell against competition. But the company has found additional ways of leveraging them. It recently signed a $16 billion cross-licensing deal with IBM, which will ensure Dell of lower cost components. Dell used its patents as collateral in the deal.[21]

The most recent example of patenting business processes – and perhaps the most far-reaching in its implications – was the granting of a patent to Amazon.com for its so-called "affiliate marketing" methods. This is a method in which any website owner can install a link to Amazon.com; the owner of the website is paid commission on any sales resulting from a customer using this link. The same process is used by many web-stores, notably Barnes & Noble, Amazon.com's arch-rival. The question arises whether Barnes & Noble – and other on-line stores using the affiliate marketing method – will now have to pay Amazon.com royalties on its use – or whether Amazon.com will take legal action to protect its patent.

Such legal action is nothing new for Amazon.com: the company had previously been granted a patent for its "one-click shopping" concept – the feature which allows a shopper with one click to place an article in his or her shopping basket. Several days after the application had been granted, Amazon.com demanded that Barnes & Noble remove their one-click shopping feature from their site. Many spectators believed that it was impossible to patent such a broadly used feature, but the courts found in Amazon.com's favor. The question is whether the courts will repeat their decision for the affiliate marketing concept. Incidentally, Amazon.com applied for these patents in 1997 – showing a remarkable foresight.[22]

What to do with printing and die-cutting

Despite the successful brain-storming session, Tom was still concerned about the future of Pieces of Fun's printing and die-cutting competence. True, there had been a large number of suggestions for new markets and much had been said about new ways of using the printing and die-cutting competence, but many of the proposed solutions involved moving Pieces of Fun into new markets of which they had little knowledge and which were already highly competitive. Was it sensible, he asked himself, to spend a large amount of time gaining access to an already crowded market? Would that result in better profits for Pieces of Fun?

With a heavy heart, he realized that there was really only one option left open to him. The technology would probably be unique for about two years. He should cash in that money now by selling the competence. He would make a deal with the buyer that for the first two years – the years when the competence would still be unique – the buyer could only use the competence to service Pieces of Fun. This would generate cash flow for Pieces of Fun and help Tom finance all the other incremental and radical innovations he had in mind. And by spinning-off the printing and die-cutting competence, he would be able to turn Pieces of Fun into a design and marketing company, instead of the manufacturing company it was at the present.

Tom had made his decision. But he still felt a little heavy-hearted. He was ultimately being forced to do something which would radically change Pieces of Fun for ever. He wondered whether anybody would ever understand…

⊔ Selling or outsourcing a competence

If there are no ways of exploiting your competence through patents, then selling or outsourcing the competence may be the way to generate cash flow with that competence.

Outsourcing has grown in importance over the last few years. And perhaps this is not least due to the incredible success of Dell Computers.

The success story of Dell has been told countless times: the 89% compounded rate of growth for several years; the sales per employee of something like $700,000. And all this in an industry which is cut-throat.

What made this happen?

One of the key factors was that Dell concentrated on creating a superb customer knowledge and support system downstream, and a shared information system that deepens its relationship with suppliers upstream. It is this process which has given Dell the edge – and a pretty big edge, too – on its competitors.

Dell has been single-minded in its approach; it has not got involved in manufacturing. Outsiders provide virtually all the competent design and innovation, software, and (non-assembly) production of its computers. The company invests only where it sees an opportunity for unique added value, and avoids the huge inventory facilities and development risks which are assumed and accepted by more integrated competitors.[23]

Many other companies are now discovering the advantages of making use of external experts. Royal Dutch Shell, for example, uses external experts to provide input for scenarios central to its strategic planning processes. Pharmaceutical companies have discovered that investing 30% of their research funds externally results in 90% of their better leads. Ford has used ABB to develop its new plants – at 70% of the internal costs these traditionally required.[24]

Ford is an example from an industry which has grown large by doing everything possible in-house. In fact, Ford is perhaps the archetypal example! Yet the company has now moved from 70% insourcing to 70% outsourcing. BMW now outsources 80% of its activities. Dell and Gateway take this even further: they go for 100% outsourcing. Even Boeing and Aerospatiale outsource almost complete electronic design and all but a few of the critical systems. The argument is that outsourcing helps tap the flexibility, expertise, and innovation of the best worldwide knowledge sources. [25]

⌐ Secure your competencies from competition

One of the questions which every manager needs to ask is "How can I secure my competencies from the competition?" Or to put it another way: how can you achieve higher sustainability?

We have written a lot about intangibles in this book. And we have tried to show how important they can be for a company. And they need protecting.

In the US, there are five means of protecting intellectual property – intangible assets which form part of a company's intellectual capital: patents, copyrights, trademarks, trade secrets, and semiconductor masks.[26]

Let us look at some of these ways individually.

Patents

As we have already seen, patents can be a powerful weapon in ensuring that competition cannot make use of your intellectual property. Xerox used patents to protect a market in which it was the only player for more than two decades. And, as we have seen, Amazon.com is using patents to combat its main competitors in e-commerce. Patents can protect both technology and business models.

Gillette is, perhaps, one of the most active users of patents to secure a permanent lead in a retail market segment. When it developed its Sensor model over ten years ago, the whole development process was aimed not only at designing a superior shaving system, but also at ensuring that key parts of the system were patented. There were seven initial designs for the new system, and a special R&D team, assisted by patent lawyers, analyzed each design and finally chose the one "that competitors would have the most difficulty getting round." The final Sensor shaving system incorporated no less than 22 patentable inventions.[27]

Trademarks

It would be hard to underestimate the value of a trademark and trade name. Not only does a trademark label the goods or services, it also adds a feeling of quality and reliability to those goods or services. Think of the value of names such as McDonald's, Sony, Nike, IBM, Coca-Cola – all evoke a whole world of perceptions and reactions. It is obvious that these trade names and trademarks should be protected, and companies register them to prevent others using them. As O'Shaughnessy and Sullivan point out: "What is there standing behind these market perceptions? A company's commercial reputation may be captured in a mark or a name just the same as an individual's personal reputation is bound inextricably with his or her name. But the trademark or name is a proxy: it captures the value of a reputation gained through the application of the firm's culture, know how, and relationships, practiced in a way that the reputation is produced. The underlying value is both created by and reposes in the firm's intellectual capital."[28]

In today's digital world, registering names becomes even more important. A young man had the foresight to register a large number of names when the internet was virtually unknown; he was later able to sell these names for enormous profits. The US government, however, did not show the same far-sightedness; the site "whitehouse.com" has nothing to do with the government of the country!

Unilever is a company with interests in a wide range of food products. One of its recent best-sellers is the "Magnum" ice-cream bar. Shortly after its highly successful introduction – it is still a brand leader in many major markets – an attempt was made to "steal" the name; Unilever had omitted to register the name in South America, and a competitor was preparing to introduce a product into the market under the Magnum name. Unilever was able to head-off this attack – but only by shipping tons of the product by plane to South America. This allowed Unilever to establish its brand in Latin America before its competitor.

With high potential profits at stake, it is not surprising that industrial espionage is assuming gigantic proportions. According to the White House Office of Science and Technology, business espionage is costing US companies something like $100 billion a year in lost sales. In a recent survey conducted by the National Counterintelligence Center and the US Department of State, it was discovered that some 74 US corporations had reported around 400 incidents of suspected foreign targeting against their businesses last year, only slightly more than half of which were engaged in producing technologies included on the NCTL.[29]

But not all espionage is sinister; competitive intelligence – the collection and analysis of public information to build up a picture of a company's competitors, customers, market, or industry – is perfectly legal. What's more, it has become a recognized weapon used by 90% of Fortune's Top 500 companies. Companies that use competitive intelligence to anticipate external forces prevent countless bad decisions, save millions of dollars, and reap advantages over current and future competitors.

BP Amoco is one of the companies which wholeheartedly embraces the use of competitive intelligence. The CEO and executive board always make use of such information when deciding on the cheapest and most effective way to enter a market.

Competitive intelligence can also save companies enormous amounts of money, as NutraSweet discovered. It had planned to launch a major offensive, costing around $86 million, aimed at positioning its brand. Competitive intelligence showed that NutraSweet's competitors were at least five years behind, and that such a brand positioning campaign was unnecessary.[30]

⌐ Anchor your competencies in the organization

It is vital that we secure the intangibles within our organization. And the first step is generally developing a plan for knowledge management.

In our previous book,[31] we described ways to manage knowledge for the purpose of creating value. One of the objectives of knowledge management is to secure the knowledge which is available throughout an organization.

Knowledge management is still, in our view, too much focussed on putting information into a database. Too often the philosophy is to get knowledge out of people's heads and put it into a computer. One may call this a "brain collecting" approach to knowledge management. This can be appropriate when the knowledge is about how to perform routine tasks – part of the knowledge involved in Tom's printing and die-cutting competence. But knowledge is seldom as simple as that. The increasing complexity of knowledge means that it does not fit easily onto digital filing cards. And then we have to wonder whether people are actually prepared to fill in such digital filing cards of their own free will. For even today, people still think that the knowledge inside their heads is their own – and need not be shared. Knowledge is still power.

In addition to the "brain collecting" approach we have long advocated the "brain connecting" approach, in which communication between people is improved, so that the sharing of knowledge becomes part of the company culture. The use of virtual communities – an ICT-enabled network of professionals with a common profession or discipline – can be instrumental in persuading people to share their views and their knowledge. By doing this, the knowledge is anchored more firmly in the organization.[32]

In our view knowledge management today also needs to go hand in hand with talent management. People are the core of most core competencies. The implicit knowledge, skills, norms, and values all reside in people. You can only anchor this sort of knowledge in your company by anchoring the people you employ.

In *The Knowledge Dividend*, we pay particular attention to what we call "smart professionals." These smart professionals are frequently at the heart of our core competencies. They are the designers who work for Tom Hoffman. Or the game developers.

Smart professionals are committed people. They are hard-working, professional, and ideal partners in your business. But they are also very well aware of their value. They do not look for life-long employment – but they are sure they will enjoy life-long employability. And this gives them a strong bargaining position. They make demands – justified demands in their eyes – for higher salaries, better employment conditions, incentives, and rewards. They know their intrinsic worth to a company – and expect the company to acknowledge that worth suitably. Smart professionals know the impact their departure can have on an organization. For they take with them all the knowledge they have, plus their own informal network which they have constructed. All too often managers are faced with clients who, thanks to this network, would prefer to do business with the departing smart professional; and in the worse scenario, clients follow the professional.

But even this is a minor danger compared to what could happen if a whole group of smart professionals were to leave together. The danger that they could set up a rival company, offering all the expertise which clients had come to expect from you, is a recurring nightmare. The number of successful small businesses and consultancies which were started in exactly this way only compounds the fear.

Any company – and particularly knowledge-intensive companies – must do everything possible to obtain a competence in attracting and retaining their smart professionals. This will include significantly increasing rewards, compensation, performance appraisal, and motivation.

Our views about motivation have changed from the simplistic to the diverse. The old "carrot and stick" method has long proved inadequate – and inappropriate – in the knowledge economy. We have also come to suspect the old idea that "a happy worker is a good worker." Today's smart professional does not need to be happy in order to work; it is the work itself which offers the greatest satisfaction.

Our old ideas about motivation seemed to have been designed for "partial people"[33]: those who do narrowly defined jobs, either routine jobs at the bottom or specialized functions at the top. But they give us little insight on how to motivate people to self management. Nor do they help us motivate people to work more closely and in greater collaboration with the people around them.

Yet there are still some CEOs of smart companies who still reach for the traditional teachings of people such as Maslow and Herzberg, ignoring the fact that what may have been successful in the industrial economy is no longer suitable to the knowledge economy. Today's new generation of smart professionals will be motivated by opportunities for self-expression and career development, combined with a fair share of the profits.[34] Today, the challenge is to motivate people to do more than their jobs.

It would be wrong, then, to assume that motivation is not recognized as the important factor it is. But as yet "no integrated theoretical framework has thus far been developed. In practice, many different approaches have been used to optimize motivation with varying degrees of success."[35] We certainly need a new motivational theory for employees working in companies with a high level of intangibles. It would need to recognize that pay and even merit pay are no longer the single driving forces for today's smart professional. Instead, it should recognize that they are motivated by opportunities for meaningful work, for which they receive recognition from management, and a fair share of the profits.

Rewarding smart professionals is a complex matter. It needs to combine all the aspects we have discussed here. But we must remember that many of these aspects are things we, as managers, have in our control. We are the ones who can show care. We can set stretching targets. We can offer the opportunities for meaningful work which smart professionals find so stimulating.

> Ultimately, knowledge management comes down to people management.

Ultimately, knowledge management comes down to people management. But people management in which concern for the individual, interest in his or her performance, care and concern, all take their proper place. As a manager, you can help motivate your staff by showing concern and care, and making them feel that their contribution is recognized and valued. When the expectations of the smart professionals are met, their skills and knowledge can be firmly anchored in the organization.

⌑ Share the knowledge, keep the talent

Tom leaned back, slightly relieved that he had finally reached a decision about the future of the printing and die-cutting competence. He knew, in his heart, that his decision to sell it was the right one. But he knew that deciding to sell and actually selling were two different matters. After all, he was selling a competence, and if he were to get a good price for it, he would have to codify the knowledge and skills which it entailed. A buyer would want to know exactly what he was getting. It was up to Tom to make sure that information was available.

As he considered the problem, he realized that he was actually thinking about knowledge management. Many of the people involved in the printing and die-cutting competence had been with the company for a long time. They had a large amount of knowledge in their heads – much of which was not committed to paper. He would need to ensure that all this "head" knowledge was made available to a new purchaser; it was, after all, one of the foundations of the competence.

Part of the success of the printing and die-cutting competence was due to the fact that it had become so embedded in the organization. And Tom realized that this was not true of the other two competencies. He wanted to increase their robustness, and he thought that a first step in the right direction would be to develop a system which would allow and encourage the sharing of knowledge. He was convinced that the game designers would automatically share their knowledge with each other – they frequently, he knew, asked each other's help on particular problems. But this sharing was not so prevalent between departments. He doubted whether the account managers were fully aware of what the game designers were doing; similarly, the game designers were often unaware of what the account managers had learned about the market. Encouraging the exchange of ideas between product portfolio management and customer management and delivery would certainly improve the synergy between the two departments. What's more, it would help develop a powerful database of knowledge which would be made available to everybody throughout the company.

And that there were good ideas in the company had become more than obvious during his brain-storming session. He had, he knew, to find a way of encouraging such a free flow of ideas and capturing that knowledge, those ideas, in a database.

But a database alone would not ensure robustness. If he wanted to leverage the "head" knowledge in his company, he would have to do his utmost to ensure that the people attached to all those heads were happy in his employment. He would have to develop new ways of keeping the talent he had in his company.

The more he thought about the problem, the more aware he became that much of his company's human resource thinking was still rooted in the production economy. They had wage scales, functional descriptions, and incremental payments. But these all stemmed from a concept that people would do a carefully prescribed job. They would need to be taught the skills needed for that job and they could depend on a good salary for their work.

But talent was another matter. How do you define the functional description for a games developer? How did you reward talent, creativity, and inspiration? Could they fit neatly into a scale?

Tom thought not.

Selling off his printing and die-cutting core competence would, in one fell swoop, transform Pieces of Fun from a manufacturing company to a design and marketing company. The old functional payment systems would no longer be relevant in this new situation.

As he thought about the new company Pieces of Fun would become in just a few months, he knew that he would need a similarly – radically – new approach to his whole human resource management.

Tom Hoffman looked out of the window in his office. It was evening, and many of the staff were leaving. He knew how they had supported the original founder of the company. How they had worked hard to make Pieces of Fun a name to be reckoned with. But he knew the future would look very different. It would have to be different. The world was changing. Changing fast. If he didn't act, the gates to Pieces of Fun might not close just at the end of the day; they might close forever.

And that was something which Tom would never allow.

7

In an article in the *Financial Times,* Baruch Lev was quoted as saying: "the way we measure the economy may have become so hopelessly outmoded by economic and technological change that an accounting revolution may be required to save it."[1]

Until now, we have concentrated on offering ways of valuing knowledge which are primarily intended for management and internal use. How can the methodology we have developed be of use for external reporting? After all, every year, millions of annual reports are produced – at an average cost of more than $30 per copy – which are intended for external reporting. A lot of money for something which is, quite simply, old-fashioned, a relic of the past, and of little use to anybody. So why do companies do it? The annual report *pur sang* is one of the only products in the world today that does not have the interests of the customer in mind. In a free market, annual reports would have no chance of survival; as it is, there is no free market, and customers are simply given the same useless information year after year.

Are we being too harsh in our judgements? We think not. In a recent article entitled "Glass Ball," Gert-Jan van Teeffelen asked: "What use are they to investors if the little information they contain is already out-of-date when they appear?"[2] And he continues: "The reporting is perhaps useful in its original form as a means of management giving its accountability to third parties (the stewardship function). But for investors, the information contained is far from adequate from the investment point of view."[3] Similar concern had already been expressed by the American Institute of Certified

Public Accountants in the so-called "Jenkins Report," which appeared in 1994. A quote from this report: "Can business reporting be immune from the fundamental changes affecting business? Can effective business reporting exclude new performance measures on which management is focusing to manage their business? In times of rapid change, the risk increases that business reporting will fall behind the pace of change, failing to provide what users need to know. Today, more than ever, business reporting must keep up with the changing needs of users or it will lose its relevance."[4]

Yet annual reports remain a bastion. A stronghold for people who believe that "things" are assets and "ideas" are expendable. It would seem that accountants have become the ostriches of today's economy. For despite all their glossy exterior, annual reports are having a measurably declining influence on the price of shares. In the 1960s and 1970s, approximately 25% of the differences in stock prices could be directly attributed to differences in reported earnings. By the late 1980s and the early 1990s, that percentage had plummeted to around 10%.[5] An annual outlay of billions of dollars to influence just a 10% fluctuation in prices!

The question arises of whether we really need to spend all this money on distributing a glossy report, containing outdated information, when alternative methods of distribution are available. Shareholders need something more than a retrospective of what has happened; they need real time reporting. With today's technology it would be quite possible to provide shareholders with a password which could give them access to a special database containing up-dated information which is relevant to them.

Already a number of companies are adopting this approach. Cisco makes its financial information available daily and on-line. And Microsoft makes its forecasts available electronically. It also publishes the assumptions used as the basis for these forecasts. Users can download the information and apply their own variables to it, thus obtaining information tailor-made to their needs.

But, as Gert-Jan van Teeffelen warns: "In the end, companies will be judged on whether they inform their stakeholders quickly and accurately. And on the confidence which they create and whether they actually deliver what they promise."[6]

Companies who bury their heads in the sand – assuming that annoying investors will simply go away – may soon be faced with the alarming reality of regulations being introduced which will require them to reveal circumstances which could have an effect on their position as a company. The London Stock Exchange is enforcing strict regulations on companies to inform investors of risks and the management of those risks. All companies listed on the London Stock Exchange will have to have an embedded internal control system that monitors on a risk-analysis basis important threats to the company. These include not only environmental, ethical, and social risks, but also risks resulting from changes in consumer behavior, supplier failure, and obsolete products. It is a recognition that a company's future depends largely on factors which are not included in the traditional balance sheet. The proposed "big bang review" requires companies to identify, evaluate, and manage significant risks and assess the effectiveness of their internal control systems.[7] As the *Financial Times* writes: "The management of companies will be held accountable for risks beyond the traditional financial threats to business."[8]

Yet there are reasons why the traditional annual report is maintained in its present form – albeit artificially.

First, the on-going globalization in many industrial and business areas brings with it the need for standardization. During the 1990s there were many efforts to adapt both national and international laws to allow a more uniform way of reporting results in different countries. This harmonization of accounting principles is a time-consuming affair and has led those involved in it to focus single-mindedly on the form – rather than taking into account the content which users now require.

Second, the users of financial reports have become increasingly diversified. And this has made them less powerful. They cannot form a united front in their demands for better – or rather, more relevant – financial reporting. And so producers of reports do not feel required to listen to their customers.

Third, the annual report in its present form is a left-over from the industrial economy. In the industrial era, there was a clear relationship between assets on the balance sheet and the results of the company. After all, in that era, stocks in raw materials, factory buildings, machinery, and capital were all indicators of future earning potential. As we have seen, times have changed – and are changing radically. In the present knowledge economy such tangible assets no longer give any guarantee of earnings and value is no longer created through transactions. In fact, we would say that in the knowledge economy, it is the intangibles which create – or destroy – value, and no transaction whatsoever is needed in this process. What's more, traditional assets wear out through transactions: your stock decreases when you sell a product, your machine wears out when producing goods. Intangibles do not wear out with use. They do not depreciate in the traditional way of tangible assets. After all, you can't wear out an idea! But this doesn't mean they retain their value indefinitely. Other forces are at work with intangibles. For example, the active use of a brand will only make its value increase. On the other hand, the arrival of a competitor who is better than you will result in a decrease in the value of your core competencies. And that is exactly why we warned in Chapter 5 that depreciation of an intangible asset is a function of your competitive advantage.

And fourth, the need to have a company's figures audited by external accountants has resulted in a large number of regulations, legal requirements, and financial conventions which greatly impairs the flexibility. What's more, regulations mean that any accountants who would want to make some remarks about intangibles – things which you cannot calculate or add up – are simply forbidden from doing so. In the traditional reporting system, most intangibles simply do not exist.

The combination of all this has resulted in something which virtually ignores the needs of its customers:

- *Timing* – the information is too late and is out of date before it is published.

- *Medium* – it appears on paper rather than on-line, even though users would much prefer the latter.

- *Focus* – it reports the past, rather than looking to the future.

- *Relevance* – it contains a lot of information which is totally irrelevant for the user.

- *Complete* – or rather incomplete, since it does not contain a lot of information which users would like.

- *Generic* – it tries to please all the people all the time – and ultimately pleases no one. No consideration is given to individual requirements of different user groups. In other words, it provides too little, too late.

You may be forgiven for thinking that we have developed the Value Explorer in an attempt to rectify this unfortunate and unsatisfactory situation. Yet that would not be the case. We did not develop the Value Explorer in an effort to improve the traditional accountancy methods; rather we developed it as a radically new way of looking at value, business methods, and – ultimately – at the way companies report their figures. It is intended as a new approach which does not look back at the traditional aspects of the industrial economy, but directs itself directly at the needs of the new knowledge economy.

⊔ Does the annual report still have a function?

In the light of everything we have said, we strongly believe that the annual report does have a function. What's more, thanks to an on-going standardization, it does allow a comparison to be made about the past performance of competing companies – even though these are based on traditional assumptions.

Our problem is that the present annual report does not meet the needs of the majority of a company's stakeholders. In today's volatile market, the value of a company is largely determined on the trading floor. Investors, market analysts, and shareholders are all interested in the future potential of a company.

One of the major problems we detect is that companies consider their annual report a "product." There are "annual report committees" and "annual report coordinators" all working to produce something glossier than the competitor.

Today we should be looking at the "function" of the annual financial reporting – or rather the various functions. Certainly the traditional function of the annual report – the accountability of management for the strategy they have followed in the past year – remains. But it can no longer stop at that. Other stakeholders in the company are making their demands. They are becoming more vocal, more prepared to speak out. And companies have to realize that this new breed of stakeholder – investors, banks, customers, suppliers, employees, and social organizations – requires a new sort of information. We cannot hope to provide these stakeholders with information which is relevant for their needs simply by repairing the accounting system developed by Pacioli. Instead, we have to develop a new system, in which the needs of these stakeholders are satisfied, both in form and content.

> **And companies have to realize that this new breed of stakeholder ... requires a new sort of information.**

But it also implies that companies wishing to give this important group the information they require will have to reveal their future plans and strategies. As the Dutch financial paper, *Het Financieele Dagblad*, pointed out: "(Shareholders) want indications about expected returns from their investments and about the risks that will be taken in order to achieve such returns. Economists prefer increasingly to look at cash flow, since accounting conventions can often give a distorted picture of such returns."[9]

Intangibles are key capital in the knowledge economy

The growth of dot.com companies, e-commerce, and e-companies show, better perhaps than anything else, how important intangibles have become in the knowledge economy. The meteoric rise in share prices of companies which have no tangible assets (except perhaps a few computers) and frequently make an enormous loss, show just how seriously the markets are now taking the whole business of intangible assets. Investors believe that such companies will enjoy a healthy cash flow in the future – and for them, this is of far greater importance than any tangible assets the company may have. Thomas A. Stewart wrote in 1995: "Some enormously successful enterprises have almost no tangible assets. A corporate metaphysician can argue, for example, that Visa International, though it processes transactions worth two-thirds of a trillion dollars a year, does not exist. Each member financial institution exclusively owns that portion of the Visa business that it has created."[10]

But despite this, intangibles are still not reported in any form.

On the surface it may seem that such reporting is of primary importance to the stakeholders in a company. Yet, as we have seen with our Pieces of Fun case, evaluating the intangibles within a company can be a highly illuminating process. Certainly it would give management a better chance to free itself from the constant pressures which are applied to achieve "shareholder value."

At the moment, such shareholder value is expressed on a balance sheet which does not take into account intangibles. In fact, as Baruch Lev writes: "Conventional accounting performs poorly with internally generated intangibles such as R&D, brands, and employee talent – the very items considered the engines of modern economic growth. Example: Today's generally accepted accounting principles call for the immediate expensing of R&D costs. But unlike rent and interest payments, intangibles often produce rich future rewards."[11] It is understandable, as the pressure on management to generate "shareholder value," that investments in R&D, training, and the like – which appear in the financial statements as expenses – are often postponed at best or neglected at worse, since they have a perceived negative effect on the demanded "shareholder value."

In other words, the present accounting practices actually promote short-term thinking and operating by managers who are under pressure to deliver shareholder value. If, however, such investments could be expressed as value to a company, then the pressure would be alleviated and management would be able to pursue a strategy of adding value to the company.

Another aspect is that it is almost impossible to calculate the return on investment (ROI) for such intangibles within the current accounting practices. These all calculate the ROI from a traditional point of view. The actual ROI could be higher or lower than originally projected.

But managers are not the only group under pressure; accountants are receiving increasing demands to report on things such as quality, management, IT structures, and other intangibles. Managers who recognize the importance of the value of intangibles for their companies frequently ask their accountants to take them into account when making up the financial statements. Accountants, so the managers reason, should help them create a balanced picture of their company – a picture in which all the tangible and intangible assets are mentioned, so that a true value can emerge. But reality shows a different picture. "American internet companies see their initial public offerings achieving enormous successes, even though many of these companies are making heavy losses. Nowhere is the difference between the market value and the book value of companies as big as with companies that work with intellectual capital. Publishers, consumer goods producers, and retailers experience a similar gap. Never before was the incompetence of accountants to value companies as visible as now."[12]

But still managers call in the help of accountants to do things above and beyond their traditional brief. Much of this, of course, is the result of the demand from interested parties not only for a more frequent flow of information, but also that the information given should cover a growing number of areas. And certainly there is a market need for such information. But there is also a danger: as the various streams of information increase, so there is a danger of those seeking information becoming swamped in the pluriformity of it all and being increasingly unable to differentiate between objective, reliable information and "spin." There is a great danger of the present "too little too late" situation turning into a "too much too soon" situation. Yet it is an area which offers enormous perspectives for accountants. There is a need to sift through the enormous amount of information being made available, so that interested parties can receive objective, reliable, and pre-selected information which is carefully geared to their needs. Jurjen Bügel summed up the situation as follows: "We are waiting for a new sort of innovation: reports on company results which go further than narrow financial reporting. Profit prognoses should be extended to include competencies and customer satisfaction. The potential of a company could then be sketched using success variables, management indicators, and technology ratings. It is in companies' own interests to provide stakeholders with a systematic review of their intangible assets and for them to make clear how these assets make a concrete contribution to adding value to the company's production processes."

Who better, one could ask, to do all this than accountants? Yet the simple fact of the matter is that under present legislation, they are not allowed to do it, even though there is a proven need for such services. It is a strange situation. But one which exists, nonetheless.

When developing the Value Explorer, we recognized that hoping to change the existing legislation would be a lengthy process and would lead to an enormous number of compromises. It would not improve the situation today – and that is why we chose to develop an instrument which would allow reporting of intangibles in a separate document which could be made available as an appendix to the existing reports, either printed or electronically. The result, however, could be that the present annual report will become even less significant than it already is today.

Despite the market demand for better information, proposals to capitalize intangible assets have generally, according to Baruch Lev,[13] been opposed by managers, financial analysts, and accountants for the following reasons:

- Intangibles are too uncertain (risky) to be considered assets.

- Amortization of the capitalized values is subjective and could be misused to manipulate financial reports.

- The costs of intangibles (the basis of capitalization) bear no relationship to their real value in light of future benefits.

- Failure of intangible projects presented on balance sheets as assets may expose managers and auditors to frivolous shareholder litigation.

It is, however, quite clear that the present situation is totally unsatisfactory. There is a need to change our way of thinking and reporting on intangibles. As venture capitalist and writer William Davidow observes: "There's a need to move to a new level in accounting, one that measures a company's momentum in terms of market position, customer loyalty, quality, etc. By not valuing these dynamic perspectives, we are misstating the value of a company as badly as if we were making mistakes in addition."[14]

Despite managerial resistance, the reporting on intangibles can serve a whole range of purposes, and it would be wrong to continue opposing this reporting. In fact, many financial managers are already involved in reporting on intangibles, even if such reporting has not yet achieved a uniformity which allows such reports to be compared with each other. Often financial managers report on intellectual capital in a variety of ways. They evaluate the progress a company is making in using its intellectual capital. They attempt to assign a value to intellectual capital for use during mergers, joint ventures, and acquisitions. They report on intellectual capital when analyzing investment proposals. They report on indicators which show how well (or poorly) a company is succeeding in increasing its intellectual capital and increasing the returns on the company's investments in that intellectual capital.

Yet while all this reporting is taking place in practice, it is still not recognized legally. The International Accounting Standards (IAS) Guidelines do not recognize the reporting of intangible assets to this extent but the IAS Committee (IASC) has formulated its conditions for valuing intangible assets in an international accounting standard – IAS 38.

It is a good initiative, yet it restricts itself to improvements within the existing system. And as we have seen, the existing system fails in so many areas that a simple fine-tuning – no matter how positive that may be – will never be sufficient. No – what is needed is a radically new way of approaching value creation in the 21st century. It is not our suggestion that we dismiss the present system out of hand; we believe there is – and will continue to be for some time yet – a place for the traditional legislation and methods. But that should not prevent us from providing the market with the information which it is increasingly demanding. Eventually, the old system may be relegated to the past – because nobody will want or need it any longer. And for this very reason, the upgrading of the present system with the sort of initiatives proposed by bodies such as the IASC will ultimately prove little more than dead ends.

⊔ Regulators want to avoid "stand-alone" actions

The case for adopting new principles for a new economy seems strong – yet there are still powerful lobbies determined to maintain the *status quo*, who want to keep the annual report in its present form. Regulators (and to a certain degree, accountants) are traditionalists, who fiercely and sometimes arrogantly defend the past, seeing little necessity for changing something they believe is more than good enough for its purpose. They seem to forget that it is not ultimately they who can or should decide what information is appropriate for the user; but it is understandable that they should suffer something approaching a cultural shock when they are brought face to face with the reality of today's world: it's a buyers' market. And buyers are becoming increasingly dissatisfied with what the sellers – the regulators and accountants – are offering for sale. As the needs of stakeholders are given more than simple lip service, sensible companies will start providing them with the sort of information which they ask – no, demand! And they will do this regardless of what regulators and accountants say.

This is no isolated phenomenon. We have already seen radical change in the labor market. Employees no longer go cap in hand to a company asking for a job; today, companies actively survey the labor market, searching for talent which they then try to win for themselves. Before the competitor beats them to it. Today's smart professionals know their worth – and hold all the trumps. The smart company is the one which understands this new situation and takes advantage of it. Regulators should follow the example of these smart companies and, rather than fighting a last-ditch battle to keep an outdated system intact, should meet the market halfway by actively trying to rid the world of the obstacles which stand in the way of accounting for intellectual capital. Simply parroting that "it can't be done" is no longer an acceptable – or tenable – position.

It is often said that valuing intangible assets amounts to little more than guesswork. It is strange that regulators should reach for this argument, for a similar case could be made against the existing methods of depreciation and matching. These methods are based on guesswork – but they have become accepted and, therefore, permissible. Furthermore, they are protected by conventions and agreements. What's more, we've always done it that way, so that makes it perfectly all right.

◻ Accountants are restricted by law

Many accountants already recognize the importance of accurate and full reporting of a company's intangible assets. But ultimately their hands are tied – by law. They are required *by law* to produce figures which can be audited. Anything which cannot be expressed objectively in financial terms has, for them – by law – no value.

But there is also a serious threat to accountants in today's changing world. At the start of the 20th century, the annual report was the major source of information for investors. Today, with the arrival of information technology, that is no longer true. Information can be gleaned from a whole range of sources. And these sources – databanks, quarterly and monthly results, and non-financial information – are far more comprehensive than the limited information found in an annual report. There is a very real threat to the accountancy profession that it will ultimately be producing a second-rate document, with little or no real value in it.

Yet it would be wrong to think that nothing at all is happening in the world of accountancy. We have already mentioned the initiatives shown in the Jenkins Report, and the work being done by Baruch Lev. There is another name we should add to the list – that of Bob Elliott. He chaired the Special Committee on Assurance Services (SCAS) of the AICPA, which has investigated the future of accountancy. This report treats the term "Assurance" in a very broad context, and takes into account new opportunities which go much further than dealing with nothing other than financial information.

⊡ Start managing and leveraging your intangibles

Until now, we have discussed external reporting on intangibles. And certainly the Value Explorer can help you measure the real return on invested capital, the development, decline, potential, sustainability, and so on of your core competencies, show ways of leveraging them, provide valuable data when making investment decisions, and accounting your actions to the stakeholders. In this light, the information it provides can be a valuable addition to the traditional annual report – but the Value Explorer was never intended to replace it.

What it can do – and do very effectively – is provide management with a vast amount of information which, until now, was largely left to the guesswork so condemned by the IASC. Paul M. Clikeman has drawn attention to the importance of knowledge and information about intangibles. In his book *Improving Information Quality*,[15] he writes: "Management decisions are only as good as the data on which they are based, and organizational misdirection due to faulty information can be costly. Therefore managers must receive relevant, accurate, and timely information at an affordable cost. After all, no organization can afford to skip evaluations that assess the quality and use of the knowledge that undergirds the business."

It is exactly here that the Value Explorer reveals its true value – by providing you with a systematic and effective way of analyzing and valuing your core competencies so that you know where to invest money to safeguard your intangibles for the future and for the benefit of future cash flow.

The whole method is based on so-called "soft" assets – things like image, culture, brand, people, and customer relationships. It can never provide a final figure which is accurate to two decimal points – but it is better to be approximately right than absolutely wrong.

When we created the instrument, a test on the reality of the figures produced was provided by an analysis of the results by corporate finance experts, who compared the figures with their own prognoses. The results did no deviate very much from each other, but the information gained provides invaluable insight into how to manage and leverage your intangible resources.

⊔ Give stakeholders the information they require

In America there is a raging debate whether reported profits bear any resemblance to the real profitability of the business. Warren Buffett, America's most admired investor, certainly does not think so. In an article in *The Economist* he said: "A growing number of otherwise high-grade managers – CEOs you would be happy to have as spouses for your children or as trustees under your will – have come to the view that it's okay to manipulate earnings to satisfy what they believe are Wall Street's desires. Indeed, many CEOs think this kind of manipulation is not only okay, but actually their duty."[16]

A duty to manipulate results? Obviously this is a situation which should be firmly condemned. Yet it is perfectly understandable. Managers are under such pressure to deliver shareholder value that it is essential for your company's survival to show you are doing just that. But this short-term thinking will not – cannot – last. Investments will have to be made. Investments in people. In knowledge. And, under the current reporting system, this will certainly not please the shareholders.

So is the answer simply *not* to invest in the tools for tomorrow's success? Obviously not. Such investments will need to be made – and they will have to be reported to the shareholders. By using the Value Explorer, such investments can be explained much more easily than with a traditional annual report. By showing the potential return on investment in intangibles – showing the value such investments can create for a company in the future – a manager is able to defend investments in intangibles and show how such investments will actually improve shareholder value. As John Kay, Britain's leading management thinker warns: "Managers … should understand two points. One is that focusing exclusively on increasing shareholder wealth may preclude you from doing things that would actually be in the long-term interests of shareholders. The second point is that adopting the shareholder priority rule not only makes it harder for you to maximize shareholder value in the long run but may also prevent you from running your business in ways everyone would agree would lead to better results."[17]

And so we have a conundrum: how to provide shareholder value now – and sustain it into the future. The secret, claim Anjan Thakor, Jeff Degraff, and Robert Quinn of the University of Michigan Business School, lies in discovering the key value drivers in the business and then tying the strategy to them. They also dispel four shareholder value myths:

- Maximizing shareholder value is created by an exclusive focus on the bottom line. Corresponding outcome: excessive focus on quarterly earnings, cost cutting, head-count slashing.

- Maximizing shareholder value means sacrificing the interest of employees and customers. Corresponding outcome: alienated customers due to poor customer service, low employee loyalty, high turnover, lost capacity.

- Giving employees shares of stock makes them act like owners. Corresponding outcome: employees typically perceive that their individual actions will minimally affect the stock price and it becomes less likely that employees behave like owners.

- The stock market is myopic and cares only about the short run. Corresponding outcome: excessive focus on intermediate financial results at the expense of sustainable and long-term value creation, including cutting back on employee development, research and development, and new product introductions.

Concentration on shareholder value may seem obligatory in a market where investors have so much influence in a market where the value of a company seems determined ultimately by the share price, not the balance sheet. Yet to pursue shareholder value at all costs – in the supposition that this creates value for your company – is short-sighted and destructive. As the *Financial Times* wrote: "Ultimately the real myth is that it is appropriate to apply generalizations about value creation to all companies, regardless of how they are strategically positioned. An exclusive focus on shareholder value may be the key to creating shareholder value for a company like Wal-Mart. It might prove to be the death-knell for an internet start-up or one like Walt Disney."[18]

> Using the Value Explorer offers you the possibility of making visible the contribution intangibles make to your profit position.

Using the Value Explorer offers you the possibility of making visible the contribution intangibles make to your profit position. And it helps you show shareholders how investments in these intangibles are being made to provide sustainable shareholder value for them. Essential investments cannot only be identified using the Value Explorer, they can also be justified to share-holders. It frees you, as manager, from concentrating on the bottom line, rather than on projected future cash flow and sustainability.

⊔ If you've got it, flaunt it

One of the criticisms we have heard about the value explorer is that publishing its results might raise a red flag to the tax authorities. These authorities could seize the information as a way of developing new means of taxation. This may not seem very feasible. Yet there is a risk if a core competence is used in a different country from that where it is located. This is a form of intra-firm trade that might be subject to tax-levy. This is one reason why multinational corporations should have a well planned and documented transfer pricing policy. Another criticism is that publishing findings revealed by the value explorer could mean giving away strategic information. We do not share this view. A true core competence – the ones we help you reveal with the value explorer – is unique to a company and cannot easily be imitated by the competition. Can another company imitate the Coca-Cola brand? Is a company culture something which another company can imitate? We do not think so.

Ultimately, successful business demands courage. Guts. The average never wins. It is the courageous players who win the prize – not the ones who sit out the game on the reserve bench. A football team doesn't keep its star quarterback under cover – it flaunts him. And successful companies are ones who dare to focus the spotlight on the star assets.

"Show your strength and others will fear you."

Using the value explorer can assist you to show your strengths.

And hopefully win.

⊔ Follow the leaders

It is our conviction that strong companies will need to take the lead. They are the ones that should be prepared to reveal their competencies and the value of their intangibles. It does, of course, require a certain strength. The revelations should not take place as a defensive ploy; rather they should be seen as a display of strength. Royal Dutch Shell has long played a leading role in the field of business principles and reporting. They have published reports in the field of ethical business practices, in the field of Health, Safety, and Environment. As yet, though, reporting on intangibles is still not common practice.

But the time may not be too far away for this to become common practice. We sincerely doubt whether companies will long be able to ignore the pressures put on them to report on intangibles. The forces of the market-place and the growing power of investors may prove too irresistible.

The days of "need to know" are numbered. Companies and managers will need to recognize this. And take steps now to move into the next age: the age of "right to know."

Appendix

The Value Explorer® toolkit

⌐ How to use the toolkit

Using the Value Explorer is all about asking new questions. The toolkit offers a set of questions which can help managers operate successfully in the knowledge economy. The toolkit consists of:

- *Steps:* a plan incorporating 15 steps which can help you in your expedition.

- *Questions:* suggestions for questions you can ask on the way.

- *Exercises:* exercises you can do alone or with others.

- *Checklists:* checklists to help you determine your core competencies' strengths and weaknesses.

- *Calculations:* a method to help you calculate the value of your intangibles.

You can use the toolkit on your own, but the results will be better if you involve others in your expedition. You could think of involving employees, customers, partners, and perhaps shareholders and financial analysts. A workshop is a good idea for certain steps – particularly when determining your core competencies. Such workshops also provide you with the opportunity to start a dialog with your colleagues and employees about the position of your company and its future. Not only will this help develop a sense of involvement among your staff, it will also help strengthen the links within your company and promote a common feeling of identity, purpose, and vision.

⊔ Phase one Examine your core

Step 1 Gathering together basic information

General information

Questions

- What were your turnover and results during the last three years?
- In what branch is your company active?
- How well known is your company and your brand?
- How would you describe your position in the market? (monopoly / large number of competitors)
- How old is your company? In which stage of the life-cycle is it?

Customer groups and needs

Questions

- What groups of customers do you serve?
- What percentage of your turnover is generated by each of these groups?
- Which percentage of this is generated by each of the groups?
- Which customer need does your company fulfill for each of these customer groups?

Market and competition

Questions

- Who are your company's competitors in today's market?
- What developments are taking place in the market?
- Which (type of) companies are likely to enter your market as newcomers?

Products and services

Questions

- Which products or services do you offer?
- What is the turnover per product / service?
- What percentage is this of the total turnover?
- What is the gross profit per product / service?

Organization and staff

Questions

- How many people work in what functions?

- Which people are essential for the continuity of your company?

- What does the organizational chart look like?

Company processes

Exercise: analyze the company processes

Describe in broad terms the processes in your company. This is very important, since it helps show in which part of the value chain the core competencies can be found. What's more, thinking about processes helps you turn a complex reality into something abstract. You should think "from outside inwards" – in other words, from end product back through the processes which lead to that end product. Try to combine as many sub-processes as possible into one main process or step in the total process. Should several main processes exist (in practice there are rarely more than five) in the company, then you should make a process description for each of these. It is important that a detailed survey is obtained of all the major processes within the company. It is not necessary to be complete and detailed. When describing the processes, the following points are of importance:

- What is the output of the company division?

- Which main processes are required for this output?

- What are the steps/stages in these processes?

- What input (knowledge, material, time) is necessary for this process?

- Which quantities can you allocate to the process (for example, turnover, costs, throughput time, number of staff, number of products)?

- Which relationships or dependencies are essential for this process?

- What are the actual essential functions (management, systems, knowledge, skills).

- How are the processes controlled?

- Which management processes (e.g. planning and control processes) are crucial for the company?

Success factors

Questions

- What makes the company successful?
- What does the company do better than other companies in the market area?
- What factors are essential for the future success of the company?

Exercise: interview your employees

People on the work floor often know a lot more about a company than management. So go and talk with ten employees and ask them about things such as:

- What are we doing right?
- What are we doing wrong?
- What complaints do our customers make?
- What is the greatest compliment you would give to our company?
- What is your major complaint?
- What is your dream for the future of our company?
- What warning would you give our company?

Step 2 Creating ideas

Look at your customers

Questions

- Why do customers like your company?
- Why do they come to you rather than choose the products or services of one of your competitors?
- What benefit do you offer to your customers that other companies apparently don't offer?
- What fundamental advantages set you apart from the rest of the field?
- Which new advantages would you like to offer your customers?
- Which competencies and skills will you need to acquire in order to offer these advantages successfully and continuously?

Exercise: interview your customers

Ask your customers directly. Preferably in a one-on-one interview situation. You should ask your customers exactly what they think the strong points of your company are. You should ask what they think should be improved. You should ask them what skills they perceive your company possessing. You should ask them where you score better than the competition – and where the competition scores better than you. Make sure the interview is carried out in an open and honest manner. Ask the interviewee to be honest. And listen carefully not just to what they say – but also to things they don't say. These are often just as illuminating.

Look at your products and services

Questions

- Do your products and services have added value?

- What advantages and benefits do your customers enjoy once they have purchased or used them?

- Do your products or services add value for your customers and help them enjoy something which they would not otherwise enjoy?

- What are the specific requirements you need to manufacture your product or offer your service?

- Are their any special skills and technologies which are demanded?

- Does the product or service require specialized knowledge?

- When you are recruiting new employees, is there a specific type of person you need?

- Do they have to have special knowledge, a specific skill, or a certain mentality?

- What are the essentials you require them to have in order for them to do the job properly?

- If one of your most important stakeholders were to call you and ask you to improve your product or service, what would be the one thing you would try to improve?

Look at your intangibles

Exercise: identify important intangibles

We know that there are a lot of intangibles in any company. But do you really know the ones which make the difference in your own? Ask yourself what they are. List them under the five categories:

Assets and Endowments:

■ What are the unique assets of your company? Think about things you have inherited from the past which have made the company what it is (customer relationships, brand awareness, etc.).

■ What value do these have in the eyes of your customers?

■ How important are they to the success of the company?

Skills and Tacit Knowledge:

■ What are the unique areas of knowledge and skills in your market? In this context, unique means differentiating.

■ What value does the client get from these?

Collective Values and Norms:

■ What are the core values shared throughout your company?

■ What norms are derived from these? (For example, the value is perfection in presentation; the norm is that any piece of correspondence is free of grammatical and typing errors.) Concentrate on the essentials and try to describe the values at the highest level of abstraction possible and try to show how various concrete norms contribute to this value. Consider the company as a whole and place the company in its proper context with its surroundings.

■ How much of this is noticed by the customer?

■ How would you describe the style of management?

■ What does management consider its prime objective?

Technology and Explicit Knowledge:

■ What systems and technologies does your company have which allows it to supply its products and services?

■ What handbooks and procedures are used within your company?

Primary and Management Processes:

■ Which primary processes are essential?

■ Which management processes (e.g. planning and control processes) are crucial for the company?

Exercise: briefing a new employee

You should also ask yourself which of these intangibles are absolutely essential within your specific branch. There's a good way of determining which of these are of primary importance. Imagine that you have employed a highly skilled professional from a different branch of industry. You have to tell this employee those things which are vital within your company. All the pieces of corporate wisdom and technical know-how which everybody in the company needs to know in order to remain successful. What would you tell your new employee? And when you tell them, which of them could be open to discussion? Which of the gems of wisdom have become folklore and have little or no significance under present circumstances? And which of these ideals could lose their relevance in the future?

Look at your competition

Questions

- Using the five categories already mentioned, what are the intangibles that make your competitor unique?

- Will the competition be able to offer products and services which are the same as yours?

- Will they be able to catch you up, or even overtake you?

- How can you improve your existing product or service offering to maintain your competitive edge?

Exercise: winners and losers

Make a list of fundamental factors which distinguish your market's winners from its losers. Again be honest with yourself and look at your company's present position. Draw up plans to eliminate the losing factors and increase the winning factors.

Exercise: collision course

List the three most dangerous courses of action your competition could take to win market share from you. Be creative. And be honest. Consider all possibilities – even those which may at present simply seem to belong to the world of fantasy. Then, once you have listed these three strategic threats, plan actions which you could take to thwart them. A further possibility here is, of course, that you come up with ideas which could be of strategic importance to you and give you an even greater lead over your competition!

Exercise: switching jobs

Imagine that you were offered the job of CEO by your leading competitor. What actions would you take in your new job to attack your previous (i.e. your present) company? Such a scenario helps expose strategic weaknesses in your present company and can help you devise improvement programs to rectify the situation before you come under attack.

Look at successful projects or product innovations

Exercise: successful products and services

Analyze successful products and services and find out what has given them their success:

■ What makes a product a success?

■ Is it because of technology?

■ Customer appeal?

■ Added benefits?

Exercise: successful projects

Look at successful projects in your company's past:

■ What contributed to that success?

■ What aspects need to be continued into the future – and what aspects need to be relegated to the past?

Landmark exercise:

List recent landmarks in your company's success story:

■ What factors have contributed to these successes?

■ Are they due to the development of a new technology?

■ The creative use of an existing skill?

■ Were they the result of an acquisition?

■ Or because you recently increased your pool of talented employees?

Exercise: product innovation

Look at your present innovations:

■ What new products and services are in the pipeline?

- Are they totally new developments – or are they a reaction to the success of a competitor?

- Do these imminent innovations add value to your company and to the way your customers benefit from using your products or services?

Look at your future

Exercise: Armageddon

Imagine that in the coming ten years your company's prospects became so bad that there is only a 10% chance that things could get any worse. You have almost hit rock bottom. Can you describe that future? Can you list internal and external causes for such a doomsday scenario? Be honest. Look failure in the face and describe the causes of that failure.

Exercise: conquest

Imagine that in the coming ten years your company's prospects improve to such a degree that there is only a 10% chance that things will improve even further. Can you describe that future? Can you list all the external causes and internal measures which will have created such a rosy future? Again be honest. Look success in the face and describe the reasons for that success.

Step 3 Defining a number of core competencies

You've completed all the preparatory work. You have now a better view of your company than you have ever had before. You know all the forces working in your market – customers, innovation, competition. You have listed intangible assets which you believe are essential for success. You know where you stand in comparison to your main competitors. Now is the time to define a number of core competencies.

Exercise: defining core competencies

- Start with "the ability to ..." Your company may have a unique ability to do something which sets you apart from the rest of the competition. Try to define this uniqueness.

- Think of a combination of skills, knowledge, processes, and culture which together form a unique competence.

- Always think of a customer benefit. You work for your customer, and a core competence should always reflect a benefit for your customer.

- Give your core competence a catchy name.

- Write down a very precise description of the core competence. The uniqueness of your company is probably founded in very subtle things. Catching this subtlety in a definition is the most important step in determining your core competencies. If you fail to do so, your competencies will be experienced by others as platitudes, cliches or trivialities that are applicable to any other company. To force yourself to be very precise you should provide definitions and synonyms for every important word in your core competence description.

Step 4 Breaking down your competence into intangibles resources

Exercise: breaking down core competencies

Break down each of the preliminary core competencies into the underlying intangibles.

When you are satisfied with the result, you can move on to the next stage: testing for strengths and weaknesses. The result could be that a core competence scores poorly on the majority of test questions. This could mean that you return to this stage to reassess your core competencies.

⊡ Phase two Assess your strengths

We have developed five checklists to help you assess your strengths and weaknesses. The results of applying the checklists to each of your core competencies will be a score between 0 and 5. The checklists will show:

- Added value

- Competitiveness

- Potential

- Sustainability

- Robustness

Step 5 Testing for added value

The factual data used for answering the questions on the added value checklist often come from customer satisfaction surveys (as described above) and from additional market analyses.

Added value checklist:

Added value	Score (1 = yes, 0 = no)
▪ The core competence offers a substantial benefit for your customers or a substantial cost-saving for your company.	
▪ Customers demand this specific benefit or cost-saving.	
▪ This benefit is important for a large number of customers; it goes further than just "nice to have."	
▪ Customers will continue expecting this benefit for the foreseeable future; it is not simply a passing fancy.	
▪ Leadership in this core competence makes customers think you are different to the competition, rather than just better.	
Total score added value:	

Step 6 Testing for competitiveness

The essential data for answering the questions on the competitiveness checklist is largely derived from competitive research, as described above, together with any further business intelligence.

Competitiveness checklist

Competitiveness	Score (1 = yes, 0 = no)
▪ Fewer than five of our competitors share this particular competence.	
▪ We are superior to our competitors in most aspects of a particular competence.	
▪ We invest substantially more time and money in this competence than our competitors do.	
▪ Our customers choose our products or services to a large extent because we have this competence.	
▪ Our leadership in this competence is generally recognized and can be illustrated with articles in trade journals, patents, and so on.	
Total score competitiveness:	

Step 7 Testing for potential

The fundamental data for answering the potential checklist is gathered through the market research described earlier, together with additional research into economic and social developments and trends.

Potential checklist

Potential	Score (1 = yes, 0 = no)
▓ There is an increasing demand for products/services which can be provided thanks to this core competence.	
▓ The core competence allows the development of new products and services in the future.	
▓ The core competence allows new markets to be entered in the future.	
▓ They are no economic threats (customers, suppliers, competitors) which will adversely affect the use of this competence.	
▓ There are no social threats (regulatory and social) which will adversely affect the use of this competence.	
Total score potential:	

Step 8 Testing for sustainability

The fundamental data for answering the sustainability checklist is gathered through the market research described earlier, together with additional business intelligence.

Sustainability checklist

Sustainability	Score (1 = yes, 0 = no)
▓ This core competence is scarce in our branch.	
▓ It would require considerable investments in time and/or money for competitors to master this competence.	
▓ Components of the competence are protected by patents, trademarks and other legal measures.	
▓ This competence is a combination of a number of intangibles such as skills, knowledge, processes, and corporate culture, thus making it difficult to copy.	
▓ This competence cannot be obtained through acquisition or from other outside sources.	
Total score sustainability:	

Step 9 Assessing robustness

The fundamental data for answering the robustness checklist is gathered through the organizational research described earlier, together with possible further internal analyses.

The following checklist deals with the vulnerability of the intangibles which contribute to the core competence. If you answer "yes" to a question, then there is a degree of vulnerability. In order to achieve a robustness score between 0 and 5, you must subtract the result achieved at the end (marked "A") from 5.

Robustness checklist

Robustness	Score (1 = yes, 0 = no)
▨ The group of people which possess the skills and knowledge crucial for this competence is vulnerable.	
▨ The values and norms on which this competence is built are under pressure.	
▨ The technology and IT systems which form part of this competence are vulnerable.	
▨ The primary and management processes which this competence uses are unreliable.	
▨ The endowments this core competence depends on (like the corporate image or the installed client base) are vulnerable.	
Total = A:	
Total score robustness: 5 – A =	

⧉ Phase three Measure your value

In order to calculate the value of your core competencies, you require information about the turnover and direct costs per product (group). The value is then calculated in six steps using this and other information. They are illustrated using the financial information of Pieces of Fun. It is useful, when making the calculations, to use a computer spreadsheet program.

Step 10 Determining gross profits

Exercise: identifying products and services

Determining the value of the core competencies starts with an analysis of the products to which the core competencies make a contribution. For convenience, you should make a list of between three and seven products or product groups. Your list should be designed so that:

- There is as broad a spread over the core competencies as possible, so that not all core competencies contribute to every product.

- It is understandable and informative.

- It matches as far as possible the structure of the figures produced by your financial administration.

Calculation: calculating gross profit per product

The gross profit is determined by deducting the direct costs from the income generated by a product. By direct costs, we mean those costs which can be directly accounted to production or service. We do not mean overheads.

A product or service is not realized solely through intangible assets, but also with tangible and financial assets, and by maintaining net working capital. Because the objective of the method is to determine a value for the intangibles alone, the gross profit must be corrected for those investments needed in order to realize a product or service. The gross profit of the products calculated is corrected by x% compensation for tangible assets, financial assets, and net working capital. You can calculate this percentage by looking at the average costs of capital in your firm.

Assets	Value	Liabilities	Value
Fixed assets	23.3	Equity	20.9
Current assets	17.6	Long-term debt	7.9
Cash	7.7	Provisions	2.9
		Current liabilities	16.9
Total	48.6	Total	48.6

Table 1 ■ Simplified balance sheet – Pieces of Fun 1999 (in US$ millions)

Fixed assets and net working capital – Pieces of Fun: US$31.7 million
Average cost of capital: 5%
Compensation for fixed assets and net working capital: US$1.6 million

	Jigsaw puzzles	Puzzle books	Board games	Computer games	Total
Sales	31.3	23.8	16.0	25.0	96.1
Direct costs	−18.9	−16.8	−14.6	−11.5	−61.8
Total	12.4	7.0	1.4	13.5	34.3
Compensation	−0.6	−0.3	−0.1	−0.6	−1.6
Gross profit	11.8	6.7	1.3	12.9	32.7

Table 2 ■ Gross profit per product – Pieces of Fun (in US$ millions)

Exercise: checking for negative results

The analysis may show that the gross profit attributed to the core competence is negative. In this case, you must determine whether this is because the core competence is at the end of its life-cycle (in which case a negative margin is correct), or at the start of its life-cycle, which means that investments so far exceed the returns. In the latter case, you need to make a prognosis of the gross profit that can realistically be expected on the basis of the future potential.

Step 11 Allocating gross profits

Exercise: creating a core competence to product matrix

The contribution of a core competence to the realization of a product always varies. The core competence can make an essential, substantial, or supporting contribution, but may also make no contribution at all. The contribution is essential if the core competence constitutes the core of the product. It is substantial if the core competence contributes to the success of the product and it is supporting if the core competence supports the realization of the product. This is shown in the competence to product matrix.

Construct a matrix in, for example, a spreadsheet, showing along the top the products, and on the left the core competencies. Indicate in each cell of the matrix the contribution each competence makes to the product, using the following table:

0 = No contribution
1 = Supporting contribution
2 = Substantial contribution
3 = Essential contribution

Add up the various columns and calculate the relative weights (in %).

Competence	Jigsaw puzzles	Puzzle books	Board games	Computer games
Printing and die-cutting	3	0	2	0
Graphic design	1	1	2	3
Intellectual entertainment	1	2	3	3
Total	5	3	7	6

Table 3 ■ Core competence to product matrix – Pieces of Fun

Calculation: allocating gross profits

Use a spreadsheet to show the relative share each competence has in the product using the previous scores.

Competence	Jigsaw puzzles	Puzzle books	Board games	Computer games
Printing and die-cutting	60%	0%	29%	0%
Graphic design	20%	33%	29%	50%
Intellectual entertainment	20%	67%	42%	50%
Total	100%	100%	100%	100%

Table 4 ■ Contribution of core competence to products – Pieces of Fun

Use these percentages to allocate the gross profits of the products to the core competencies.

Competence	Jigsaw puzzles	Puzzle books	Board games	Computer games	Total	%
Gross profit (see table 2)	11.8	6.7	1.3	12.9	32.7	
Printing and die-cutting	7.1	–	0.4	–	7.5	23
Graphic design	2.4	2.2	0.4	6.4	11.4	35
Intellectual entertainment	2.4	4.4	0.6	6.4	13.8	42
Total	11.8	6.7	1.3	12.9	32.7	100

Table 5 ■ Allocation of gross profit to core competencies – Pieces of Fun (in US$ millions)

Step 12 Determining potential

Calculation: determining potential

The potential of the core competence is shown as a percentage of the expected growth per year of the gross profit. This growth can be determined using market analyses which predict the growth in turnover and the costs and thus the growth in gross profit. These growth percentages can then be used to calculate the expected growth in the gross profit per core competence. Of course, you must take into account when calculating this, the relative importance of each core competence as determined in Table 5.

In the following table, we have used a growth percentage for four products of Pieces of Fun, of respectively –4%, 0%, –3%, and 24%. Using this we can calculate the expected gross profit for the next year. This gross profit is then distributed over the various core competencies in the same way as in Table 5. By comparing the results with those of the previous year, we can calculate a growth percentage per core competence. This is the potential factor.

	Jigsaw puzzles	Puzzle books	Board games	Computer games	Total 2000	Total 1999	Change	Potential (%)
Gross profit 1999	11.8	6.7	1.3	12.9				
Annual growth rate	–4%	0%	–3%	24%				
Gross profit 2000	11.3	6.7	1.3	16.0				
Printing and die-cutting	6.8	–	0.4	–	7.2	7.5	0.3	–4
Graphic design	2.3	2.2	0.4	8.0	12.8	11.4	1.4	13
Intellectual entertainment	2.3	4.4	0.6	8.0	15.3	13.8	1.4	10
Total	11.3	6.7	1.3	16.0	35.3	32.7	2.6	8

Table 6 ■ Determining potential percentage based on an annual growth rate per product (amounts in US$ millions)

Step 13 Estimating sustainability

Calculation: estimating sustainability

The sustainability of a core competence is equal to the number of years a company can enjoy a lead with it. This is sometimes hard to calculate. In our experience, the predictions for sustainability produced by market analysts are highly variable, which often makes them less usable. Therefore we use as the number, the number of questions answered positively in the Sustainability checklist. Using this method increases the comparability of the results and offers a standardized way of calculating sustainability.

Competence	Sustainability score	Number of years sustainable
Printing and die-cutting	2	2
Graphic design	1	1
Intellectual entertainment	3	3

Table 7 ■ Sustainability of core competencies – Pieces of Fun

Step 14 Assessing robustness

Calculation: assessing robustness

There are very sophisticated methods for calculating risks. Most, however, are highly complicated and offer too much "overkill" to be suitable here. For this reason, we have adopted a pragmatic and simple calculation method here: each risk identified in the robustness checklist increases the chance of losing the core competence by 20%.

Competence	Robustness score	Robustness
Printing and die-cutting	5	100%
Graphic design	3	60%
Intellectual entertainment	5	100%

Table 8 ■ Robustness of core competencies – Pieces of Fun

Step 15 Calculating value

You have now gathered all the information you need for calculating the value of your core competencies. It may sound complicated, but the value of a core competence is equal to the net present value of the gross profit which is generated during the period of sustainability of the competence, corrected with a factor for robustness.

Let's take this one step at a time.

Exercise: create timetable

Start with your first core competence. Refer now to the figure you have calculated for sustainability (see Table 7). Make a table with, in the first column, the years which count when determining the present value. Tom Hoffman used figures about gross profit from the 1999 book year. The sustainability for the core competence printing and die-cutting is two years. And so, for this competence, to calculate the present value Tom is allowed to include the expected gross profit for the years 2000 and 2001.

Calculation: calculating future gross profit

Now calculate for these years the gross profit using the gross profit in the chosen book year and the expected growth per year as calculated with the Potential % (see Table 6).

Year	Contribution to gross profit
1999	7.5
2000	7.2
2001	6.9

Table 9 ■ Future gross profit of the Printing and die-cutting competence – Pieces of Fun (in US$ millions, Potential = –4%)

Calculation: calculating present value

This gross profit must now be turned into a present value. For this, we use a discount factor which is the same as the average cost of capital.

Year	Gross profit	Discount factor of 5%	Present value
2000	7.2	95.2%	6.9
2001	6.9	90.7%	6.2
Total			13.1

Table 10 ■ Present value of the Printing and die-cutting competence – Pieces of Fun (in US$ millions)

Calculation: incorporate robustness

Multiply the present value of the core competence with the factor for Robustness (see Table 8).

Present value	13.1
Robustness	100%
Value	13.1

Table 11 ■ Value of the Printing and die-cutting competence – Pieces of Fun (in US$ millions)

Calculation: calculating the total value of your intangibles
Finally: make a table showing the values of the core competencies, their relative shares, and the total value of your intangibles.

Competence	Value	%
Printing and die-cutting	13.1	20%
Graphic design	7.4	11%
Intellectual entertainment	45.5	69%
Total	66.0	100%

Table 12 ■ Total value of the intangibles of Pieces of Fun (in US$ millions)

Notes

Chapter 1

1 Meyer, C, and David, S (1998) *Blur*. Capstone Publishing Ltd.

2 Stewart, TA "Brain Power: Who owns it and how they profit from it," *Fortune*, 135(5), March 17, 1997.

3 Davenport, TH and Prusak, L (1998) *Information Ecology*. Oxford University Press.

4 "The NIKE Story? Just tell it!," *Fast Company*, January–February 2000.

5 "Secrets of Fortune's Fastest-Growing Companies," *Fortune*, 140(5), September 6, 1999.

6 Meyer, C, and David, S (1998) *Blur*. Capstone Publishing Ltd.

7 "America's Fastest Growing Companies," *Fortune*, 143(7), October 14, 1996.

8 Stewart, TA (1997) Doubleday/Currency, *Intellectual Capital*.

9 *Financial Times*, July 28, 1997.

10 Mavrinac, S, and Siesfeld, GA (1998) "Measures That Matter: an exploratory investigation of investors' information needs and value priorities," *The Economic Impact of Knowledge*. Butterworth-Heinemann.

11 Meyer, C, and David, S (1998) *Blur*. Capstone Publishing Ltd.

12 Ibid.

13 Edvinsson, L, and Malone, MS (1997) *Intellectual Capital*. HarperCollins Publishers, Inc.

14 Baruch Lev, "The Old Rules No Longer Apply," *Forbes*, April 7, 1997.

15 Ibid.

16 Skyrme, DJ "Valuing Knowledge: Is it worth it?," *Managing Information*, 8(3), March 1998.

17 Stewart, TA (1995) "Trying To Grasp The Intangible," *Fortune*, 132(7).

18 Davidow, W (1993) *The Virtual Corporation*. Harperbusiness.

19 Donaldson, TH (1992) *The Treatment of Intangibles*. St. Martin's Press.

20 Lekanne Deprez, FRF and Haak, TW (1999) "Individual Balanced Scorecards, Capitalizing on Individual and Organizational Needs for Mutual Benefit," *Rethinking Knowledge*.

21 Skyrme, DJ "Valuing Knowledge: Is it worth it?," *Management Information*, 5(2), March 1998.

22 Kelly, J, "Corporate Reporting, User Unfriendly," *Financial Times*, January 4, 1999.

Chapter 2

1 Stewart, TA (1997) *Intellectual Capital*, Doubleday / Currency.

2 Sullivan, PH (1998) *Profiting from Intellectual Capital*. John Wiley & Sons Inc.

3 Ibid.

4 Ibid.

5 Tissen, R, Andriessen, D, and Lekanne Deprez, F (2000) *The Knowledge Dividend*. Financial Times Prentice Hall.

6 Roos, J, Roos, G, Edvinsson, L and Dragonetti, NC (1998) *Intellectual Capital: Navigating in the new landscape*. New York University Press.

7 Ellis, J (1999) *Doing Business in the Knowledge Based Economy*. Pearson Education.

8 Roos, J, Roos, G, Edvinsson, L and Dragonetti, NC (1998) *Intellectual Capital. Navigating in the new landscape*. New York University Press.

9 Ibid.

10 Ellis, J (1999) *Doing Business in the Knowledge Based Economy*. Pearson Education.

11 Roos, J, Roos, G, Edvinsson, L and Dragonetti, NC (1998) *Intellectual Capital. Navigating in the new landscape*. New York University Press.

12 Kaplan, RS and Norton DP "The Balanced Scorecard – Measures that drive performance," *Harvard Business Review*, January–February 1992.

13 Ibid.

14 Ibid.

15 Sveiby, KE "The Balanced Score Card (BSC) and the Intangible Assets Monitor," http://203.32.10.69/IntangAss/ImagesIntangAss/BSCandIAM.html

16 Ibid.

17 *Celemi Intangible Assets Monitor*. Celemi International AB. 1997.

18 DeSouza, G, "Royalty Methods for Intellectual Property," *Business Economics*, April 1997.

19 *Human Resource Accounting: A practical business economic perspective?* ("Human Resource Accounting, een werkend bedrijseconomisch perspectief?"), Bulte, J, Stenfer Kroese BV, 1975.

20 Ibid.

21 Lev, B, "New Math for a New Economy," *Fast Company*, January / February 2000.

Chapter 3

1 de Geus, A (1997) *The Living Company*. Harvard Business School Press.

2 Hamel, G and Prahalad, CK (1994) *Competing for the Future*. Harvard Business School Press.

3 Ellis, J (1999) *Doing Business in the Knowledge Based Economy*. Pearson Education.

4 Capodagli, W and Jackson, L (1999) *The Disney Way: Harnessing the management secrets of Disney in your company*. McGraw-Hill.

5 Dr Javidan, M (1998) "Core Competencies: What they mean in practice," *Long Range Planning*, 31(1).

6 Capodagli, W and Jackson, L (1999) *The Disney Way: Harnessing the management secrets of Disney in your company*. McGraw-Hill.

7 Ibid.

8 Ibid.

9 Ibid.

Chapter 4

1 *New York Times*, December 20, 1998.

2 Kelly, K (1998) *New Rules for the New Economy*. Viking Penguin Group.

3 Hamel, G and Prahalad, CK (1994) *Competing for the Future*. Harvard Business School Press.

4 Ibid.

5 Ibid.

6 "ING Barings Loses Team Of Exchange Dealers" (ING Barings raakt team effecten handelaren kwijt). *Het Financieele Dagblad*, April 1, 1996.

7 Chaterjee, S, "Delivering Desired Outcomes Efficiently: The creative key to competitive strategy," *California Management Review*, Winter 1998.

8 Dr Javidan, M (1998) "Core Competencies: What they mean in practice," *Long Range Planning*, 31(1).

9 Long, C and Vickers-Koch, M,"Using Core Competencies to Create Competitive Advantage" *Organizational Dynamics*, Summer 1995.

10 Dr Javidan, M (1998) "Core Competencies: What they mean in practice," *Long Range Planning*, 31(1).

11 Coyne, K (1997) "Is Your Core Competence a Fata Morgana?" *The McKinsey Quarterly*, 1.

12 Dr Javidan, M (1998) "Core Competencies: What they mean in practice," *Long Range Planning*, 31(1).

13 "Irrepressible Irrelevant," *The Economist*, February 6, 1999.

14 David, S, and Meyer, C (1998) *Blur*. Capstone Publishing Ltd.

15 Björk, S (1998) "Ikea: Entrepenören, affarsiden, kulturen." *Svenska Förlaget*.

16 Galagan, PI "Strategic Planning is Back," *Training and Development*, April 1997.

17 Dr Tampoe, M (1994) "Exploiting the Core Competencies of Your Organization," *Long Range Planning*, 27.

18 Ibid.

19 Kesler, M, Kostad, D and Clarke, WE, "Third Generation R&D, The key to leveraging core competencies," *The Columbia Journal of World Business*, 28(3).

20 Hall, L. (1992) "Strategic Analysis of Intangible Resources," *Strategic Management Journal*, 13; Hall, L (1993) "A Framework Linking Intangible Resources and Capabilities to Sustainable Competitive Analysis," *Strategic Management Journal*, 14; both quoted in Harvey, M, and Lush, R (1997) "Protecting the Core Competencies of a Company: Intangible asset security," *European Management Journal*, 15(4).

21 "ING Barings Loses Team Of Exchange Dealers" (ING Barings raakt team effecten handelaren kwijt), *Het Financieele Dagblad,* April 1, 1996.

22 Simons, R, 'How Risky is Your Company?' *Harvard Business Review,* May–June 1999.

23 Ibid.

Chapter 5

1 Strassman, P, "Measuring and Managing Intellectual Capital," *Knowledge Inc.,* June 1999.

2 Donaldson, TH (1992) *The Treatment of Intangibles.* St Martin's Press.

3 Birchard, W, "Intangible Assets + Hard Numbers = Soft Finance," *Fast Company,* October 1999.

4 Ibid.

5 Quoted in Roos, G and Roos, J (1997) "Measuring your Company's Intellectual Performance," *Long Range Planning,* 30(3).

6 Birchard, W, "Intangible Assets + Hard Numbers = Soft Finance," *Fast Company,* October 1999.

7 Ibid.

8 Copeland *et al.* (1990) *Valuation; Measuring and managing the value of companies,* John Wiley & Sons.

Chapter 6

1 Markides, C, "Strategic Innovation," *Sloan Management Review,* Spring 1997.

2 Kawasaki, G and Moreno, M (1999) *Rules for Revolutionaries.* HarperCollins Publishers Inc.

3 "Box Suppliers Turn to Services," Henny van der Pluijm ("Dozenschuivers gaan in diensten") *Intermediar,* March 25, 1999.

4 Padgett, N (1998) "Night Vision comes to Cadillac," *Automobile Industries,* 178(9).

5 Kawasaki, G and Moreno, M (1999) *Rules for Revolutionaries.* HarperCollins Publishers Inc.

6 "Strategic Management of Intellectual Property: Enhancing organizational success by unlocking the value of ideas." KPMG Intellectual Property Portfolio Service.

7 Adapted from a variety of sources, including: "Rough Ride," *The Economist,* November 14, 1998; "A Handbrake on Subsidies," *The Economist,* February 13, 1999; "When Crashing is Not an Option," *The Economist,* November 28, 1999; "Microsoft joins forces with Ford to sell cars online," *FEMDeDag,* September 21, 1999.

8 Kelly, K (1998) *New Rules for the New Economy,* Viking Penguin Group.

9 Adapted from a variety of sources: "Buying an Experience," Peter Martin, *Financial Times,* September 14, 1999; "The Revolution at Ford," *The Economist,* August 7, 1999; *FEMDeDag,* August 5, 1999.

10 Kim, W Chan and Mauborgne, R, "Creating New Market Space," *Harvard Business Review,* January–February 1999.

11 Bloomberg and Philips Lighting Company cases adapted from Kim, W Chan and

Mauborgne, R, "Creating New Market Space," *Harvard Business Review*, January–February 1999.

12 Kim, W Chan and Mauborgne, R, "Creating New Market Space," *Harvard Business Review*, January–February 1999.

13 Case adapted from Kim, W Chan and Mauborgne, R, "Creating New Market Space," *Harvard Business Review*, January–February 1999.

14 Kim, W Chan, and Mauborgne, R, "Creating New Market Space," *Harvard Business Review*, January–February 1999.

15 Case adapted from Kim, W Chan and Mauborgne, R, "Creating New Market Space," *Harvard Business Review*, January–February 1999.

16 Examples taken from Eccles, RG, Lanes, KL and Wilson, TC "Are You Paying Too Much For That Acquisition?," *Harvard Business Review*, July–August 1999.

17 IFI Plenum Data Corporation, Wilmington, NC, 1998.

18 Rivette, KG and Kline, D, "Discovering New Value in Intellectual Property," *Harvard Business Review*, January–February 2000.

19 Ibid.

20 Ibid.

21 Ibid.

22 *FEMDeDag*, February 28, 2000.

23 Quinn, JB "Strategic Outsourcing: Leveraging Knowledge Capabilities," *Sloan Management Review*, Summer 1999.

24 Ibid.

25 Ibid.

26 Sullivan, PH (1998) "Extracting Value from Intellectual Assets" in Sullivan, PH (ed) *Profiting from Intellectual Capital*, John Wiley & Sons.

27 Rivette, KG and Kline, D, "Discovering New Value in Intellectual Property," *Harvard Business Review*, January–February 2000.

28 O'Shaughnessy, J, and Sullivan, PH "The Role of Intellectual Capital in Valuing Knowledge Companies" in Sullivan, PH (ed) *Profiting from Intellectual Capital*, John Wiley & Sons.

29 "Economic Espionage", http://www.asisonline.org/stat3.html

30 Adapted from "Legal Espionage," *CIO Enterprise Magazine*, July 15, 1998.

31 Tissen, R, Andriessen, D and Lekanne Deprez, F (2000) *The Knowledge Dividend*. Financial Times Prentice Hall.

32 Ibid.

33 Maccoby, M (1988) *Why Work? Motivating and leading the new generation*. Touchstone/Simon & Schuster.

34 Tissen, R, Andriessen, D and Lekanne Deprez, F (2000) *The Knowledge Dividend*. Financial Times Prentice Hall.

35 van Breukelen, W and van der Vlist, R, "Motivation, Work, and Organizational Psychology," *De Psycholoog*, February 1997.

Chapter 7

1 Leadbetter, C, "Why the Traditional Methods May Have Had Their Day," *Financial Times*, April 1999.

2 van Teeffelen, G-J, "Glass Ball" (Glazen bol), *De Volkskrant*, October 2, 1999.

3 Ibid.

4 *Improving Business Reporting: A customer focus, meeting the information needs of investors and creditors*, The American Institute of Certified Public Accountants, 1994.

5 Baruch Lev, "The Old Rules No Longer Apply," *Forbes*, April 7, 1997.

6 van Teeffelen, G-J, "Glass Ball" (Glazen bol), *De Volkskrant*, October 2, 1999.

7 *Internal Control, Guidance for Directors on the Combined Code*, The Institute of Chartered Accountants, September 1999.

8 "Companies Face Tough Rules on Risk Management," *Financial Times*, September 27, 1999.

9 "Financiers Want More Insight into a Company's Future" (Financier wil meer zicht op toekomst bedrijf), *Het Financieele Dagblad*, August 8, 1997.

10 Stewart, TA "Trying to Grasp the Intangible," *Fortune*, October 2, 1995.

11 Baruch Lev, "The Old Rules No Longer Apply," *Forbes*, April 7, 1997.

12 van Empel, F, "Only People on the Balance" ("Alleen nog maar mensen op de balans"), *Next*, July/August 1999.

13 Baruch Lev, "The Old Rules No Longer Apply," *Forbes*, April 7, 1997.

14 Davidow, W (1993) *The Virtual Corporation*. HarperBusiness.

15 Clikeman, PM "Improving Information Quality," *Internal Auditor*, June 1999.

16 "Think of a Number," *The Economist*, September 11, 1999

17 "Shareholders Aren't Everything," *Fortune*, February 17, 1999.

18 "Creating Sustained Shareholder value and Dispelling Some Myths," *Financial Times*, November 15, 1999.

Company index

Name index

Subject index